Based on true events

My Money Tree

Contents

Foreword

Hello. I shall keep this short and sweet because let's be fair, who ever reads the foreword? It's usually boring and we skip it. My name is Kate. Kim and I collaborated to write this book and all we ask is for you to read and enjoy. I've known Kim since I was eight years old because my mother fell in love with her father, consequently becoming my step-dad – well, Dad. Anyway, when Kim was first in the public eye and appeared on ITV's This Morning, we weren't in touch. I had fallen out with her a few years before and chose to 'block her' over something silly. I live in Spain and didn't have British channels, so being the nosey bastard I am, I looked up the interview on the internet and sure enough her television debut was there.

I called for my daughter to come and watch it, "Quick, Scarlett, Aunty Kimmy is on the telly." We watched it together.

"Next she'll be on Celebrity Big Brother and will be writing a book," I said.

"Why don't you write it for her, Mum?" said Scarlett and that was that, I thought nothing more of it. Then a few years later, Kim discovered social media and sent me a friend request and we began to talk, then a few months later she sent me a text message and the messages were like this...

"Kate, I've got a brilliant idea and I need your help!"

Alarm bells went off in my head as I was accustomed to her brilliant ideas and get-rich-quick-schemes and replied, "If it's a get-rich-quick-system, I haven't got any cash, so I am not interested but will always give you my advice."

"No it's nothing like that, I want to write my memoir," she replied.

"Cool, there are people that can do that for you, ghost writers," I replied.

"No my agent tried writing a bit and it just sounds boring, I need someone that knows me to write it," she said. "I want you to write it."

Well I was shell-shocked and wasn't sure I was capable of doing it. Being the grown up that I am, I asked advice from my twenty two year old daughter, "What d'you reckon Scarlett? Kim wants me to write her book?"

"Do it Mum, you can do it."

So I accepted the challenge.

Damn, I thought after. Why had I agreed to write her book? I had written my own memoir a few years ago but writing for someone else? I wasn't sure I could do it. I will admit that it took me a while to get focused, months even. There was always something happening with family arriving in the summer, then my husband's surprise fiftieth birthday party, then Christmas so I put the book on the backburner. But eventually I did get focused and here is the book.

All I would like to say is thank you to Scarlett for believing in me and thank you to my two Rafas - husband and son - for tolerating me moaning when I was trying to write and they were being noisy. "Will you both shut up, I am trying to concentrate here," I would often say. Nobody moaned when they came home and the house was unclean because I had spent the entire day writing in my pyjamas from the night before.

Once I got into it, I enjoyed writing Kim's memoir because I knew most of the characters in the book. Some parts were doubly funny for me and thank you Kim for being so patient. You never pressurised me in finishing this book.

My Money Tree
Kim Farry

Chapter 1 - The early years

"Quality, mate" (in a strong cockney accent, followed by a high screeched pitch of laughter). Yes, that's, me. My name is Kim Farry and this is my story.

The irony of it is that "quality mate" is one of my favourite sayings (along with many others, most of which start with the F-word), but as a child we certainly didn't have a lot of quality about - just quantity. Kids, kids and kids, I was surrounded by siblings. I was the eldest of nine children and, as the saying goes, without a pot to piss in.

My earliest memories date back to when I was around two or three years old and lived in Surbiton, Surrey, opposite a school. I was the eldest followed by my sister Sylvia, and brothers Patrick and Scott. The place was very old fashioned and by today's standards probably uninhabitable. I don't remember much but the kitchen cupboard was free standing and we had an old fashioned larder with cupboards and drawers. The front room had an armchair near to the door which opened onto the small hallway, just big enough for one person to pass through towards the front door. We didn't have beds, just mattresses on the floor and our very own pet rats. You could hear them scurrying across the floors at night, Dad would launch his shoes at them shouting "Bloody rats!"

That armchair in the front room held a special meaning to me. It was my "Daddy" chair. Dad was forever trying to teach me the time and would show me the clock, "Right Kimmy, when the big 'ands on twelve an' the little 'en is on the six, it's when I'm 'ome," he'd say. Oh I'd get it okay, I worshipped my Daddy. He wasn't a big man, but handsome from Irish stock. Both his parents had emigrated from Northern Ireland many years ago. He was a proud man with a gruff voice and a very contagious laugh.

So anyway, I had an evening ritual. As I watched the clock approach "Daddy time", I would climb onto the armchair and upon hearing him open the door, I'd jump from the armchair into his arms. Each night he would catch me saying "Hello Daddy's little angel" and give me a huge kiss and cuddle. This continued until I was about five years old. I never forget that day when this all changed. There was a knock at the door, I assumed it was Daddy, so I climbed onto the chair getting ready to jump. Only this time, unbeknown to me, it wasn't Daddy, so I jumped with nobody to catch me. I smashed my face on the floor and was in a bloody mess.

In fact, knocking the door were the police who informed my Mum that Dad had that day received a prison sentence after committing a petty crime and would not be returning home for a while. Suffering from shock Mum had completely forgotten about my evening ritual and failed to catch me. I guess that's when I developed my trust issues and began doubting Mum. She obviously didn't tell me he had gone to prison, just that he would be working away for a while.

I wasn't a particularly mischievous child, just very, very strong willed and very determined. If I got an idea into my tiny head, I would have to pursue it. One night whilst everyone else was sleeping, I decided to creep downstairs and make myself breakfast, well, more like a midnight feast. So I climbed onto the giant free standing larder and to my horror, it proceeded to topple over landing on top of me. There was an almighty bang as plates, cutlery and food went flying everywhere, some smashing into pieces, and the entire household awoke. I crawled out from under the rubble and more afraid of the consequences of my actions but thankfully Dad was fine, he just checked that I was alright and had no injuries. There wasn't a scratch on me.

Patrick, my baby brother, became my very own living doll who I loved to dote on, but my mischevious self had wanted this to be a reality and one day, I turned him into a baby sister. I was probably aged five and I was determined to choose a little dress for him to put on. Unsure about the footwear, I went with the red wellington boots. I still wasn't satisfied with the results and felt he needed something more. Ah, I know, pink hair. So I got the Windolene from under the sink and smothered it into his hair until it was pink. Then I took him on a trip to the local sweet shop ensuring I held his little hand firmly all the way, like a good mummy. I'm not quite sure what the owners of the sweet shop thought. They were both incredibly small, my height, they must have been dwarfs, but I just assumed they were little like me.

Mum as usual went crazy, not just because we had gone missing to the shop but it took her hours trying to wash the Windolene out of Patrick's hair. I used to disappear on my own frequently. I hated being cooped up indoors. I was, and still am, a very stubborn girl, but also possessed a sweet quiet nature with an angelic smile, a cutie, all of Dad´s friends had a soft spot for me.

My stubbornness caused a bit of a tiff one Christmas when Sylvia and I both received dolls' prams, her's was blue, and mine was beige. Well, without sounding too ungrateful, I didn't want the bloody beige one. Beige was not my colour, I wanted the blue one. I caused such a drama over the fact that I didn't want the beige pram that eventually mum decided that we would swap prams so Sylvia had mine. I know that makes me sound like a bit of a brat but it was the principle of the matter.

We managed to upgrade from the tiny rat infested place in Surbiton and moved to 85 Porchester Road in Kingston upon Thames. Not only did our house appear upgraded, we had grown in numbers too, now I had not three siblings but seven. We had become a clan. I was the eldest, then Sylvia, Patrick, Scott, Tracy, Lee, Robbie and Tammy. I adored being a second "Mummy" to my siblings and loved the new three bedroom terraced house. It backed onto the railway line for the trains that went from Kingston to Waterloo and the house would tremor if any fast trains passed through. But as anyone who has ever lived near a railway line would know, you soon become accustomed to the noise. Mind you, the noise from all of us kids probably disturbed the commuters. It was by no means a quiet household, kids fighting, kids laughing, kids crying, kids whining and good old

Mum puffing away like a steam engine on 60 Number Ten cigarettes a day.

We were poor, but hey this is the 1970s we are talking about. It seemed that all of our neighbours were poor too. We were all pretty much living on the poverty line. Most families had just a few children but there were a few large ones like ours. I could never quite fathom that, why have so many children when you have no money? I often overheard my parents arguing about money, Mum spoke softly but Dad would raise his voice.

"Money don't grow on fuckin' trees!" he would yell.

During autumn, when golden leaves would fall onto the path, I used to scoop them up in my arms and pretend that the leaves were money - my money trees.

Our furniture was all second hand and very sparse. Judging by the rickety and scratched kitchen table, it wobbled so much, one leg had a piece of cardboard stuffed under it to stop our dinner plates from flying off, probably 20th hand. See we weren't that poor, we had a few plates!

The house was gloomy. No central heating for us, just a coal fire that we all huddled round. To me, it seemed to be the only thing in the house that cheered the place up. I would stare into the flames and for those moments that

I gazed at it, felt like escapism from the dreariness that surrounded us. I would daydream whilst consumed by the magical flames, then bang, back to reality. But there was not always money for coal so it would be coats worn inside, huddled under blankets as we tried to get a glimpse of the black and white wooden television.

Sometimes Mum would burn anything to keep warm. If she spotted some abandoned furniture she would send us kids out to fetch it to chop it up and throw it on the fireplace. We joked, "Shit, you'd better sleep with your shoes on tonight or Mum'll burn 'em". But she had been known to burn a few pairs of shoes.

The television was wooden and had a huge dial to change the channels. I recall having BBC1, BBC2 and ITV. It had a huge aerial sitting on top and the screen was forever rolling upwards at which point one of us would get up, bang it on the top to try and stop the rolling effect, then another would be prancing around with the aerial in their hand lifting and lowering it trying to get a better picture. A small screen with nine kids craning their necks to get a glimpse of Andy Pandy, I usually gave up and began to daydream. I swear it was like a mini workout with that bloody television. We spent more time banging it and rotating the aerial into different positions that we did watching the wretched thing. Then of course, we had to play hide and seek when the television license man knocked on the door. We had to shut the doors, lay low and keep quiet until he had left, praying the little ones wouldn't make a sound. It wasn't the only man we were taught to hide from; there was also the tallyman that visited the house.

I kind of knew from an early age that our family struggled to make ends meet, but it wasn't just us. Many neighbours had the same predicament, living hand to mouth. Struggling to survive and one way to survive was to have the tallyman. By way of the tallyman it meant that when strapped for cash, Mum could borrow money to buy things then pay him back on a weekly basis with high interest rates - a bit like today's loan sharks. Our particular tallyman was Rosenna, a peculiar looking man with pointed features - a very long nose, and he always wore a black hat, a bit like the penguin from Batman. He looked scary, so we invented a song to taunt him each time he visited.

"Rosenna are you cleaner, do you smell, smell, smell? Are you well, well, well?" Then we would run away giggling away at our hilarious song like the little fuckers that we were.

Payday for Rosenna was usually every Friday, but on one particular Friday, Dad happened to be home and gave Rosenna a volley of abuse about how he preyed on poor and vulnerable housewives to line his own pockets, blah, blah, blah. He must have given him quite a fright because that was the last time he ever came knocking. When Dad's Irish temper came out, everyone hid for cover. He could be very scary at times.

Hygiene was not a priority in our household. In the bathroom sat two toothbrushes along with the cheapest of toothpaste, a bar of cheap soap and a bottle of Tesco's family shampoo. I didn't know what hair conditioner was, none of us did until we grew up. It was a case of "the care bears, caring is sharing," that meant the bath water too. We bathed once a week but as the eldest, I made it damn sure that I went first. That was my birth right. It was so cold in the winter that you could see your breath in the bathroom so not a great incentive to strip naked a take a bath. As for sharing a toothbrush with everyone I would use my finger as I felt that was more hygienic.

Housework was not one of my Mum's greatest skills and the house always seemed dirty. I suppose when you have nine children to look after there is not much time left to clean the house. Us older kids always helped with the younger ones. We changed their nappies, wiped their snotty noses, comforted them when they were sad and teased them. I was mummy Kim for many years. Whilst Mum was preoccupied with the smaller children I would help out with the middle ones. They would come to me with their worries and fears and I would try and console them. No mod cons for us meant that we didn't have a washing machine so Mum would wash everything by hand in the kitchen sink which also doubled as a baby bath. A few of my siblings were bed wetters so the smell of urine lingered in the bedrooms.

Since a very small child I was deaf in one ear, and partially in the other. Nobody realised for a long time because I self-taught myself to read people's lips. They say that when one of your senses is lacking others become stronger and in my case this is particularly true because I have a very strong sense of smell and a built-in ability to sense danger (not quite sure that is connected) and was sensitive to the odours coming from the dirty washing cupboard. I used to wretch at the stench of it.

Porchester Road was full of kids playing. Snotty nosed dirty looking little urchins, all thrown out to play all day. We were called in at mealtimes and when the street lights came on in the summer months. Not many Dads had cars then - I say Dads because I don't recall any of the

Mums learning to drive. They couldn't afford cars so there was barely any traffic down our road. The entire road was ours to play whatever we wanted, football, tennis, we would just move to one side if the occasional car drove by.

There were also spitting contests to see who could spit the furthest. I wasn't obviously a boy, but enjoyed playing football with them. The girls like to play French skipping with elastic round our ankles - one of us at each end stretched out the elastic so it formed two low down rows and a third girl would jump in and out while we sang strange songs. One went, "England, Ireland, Scotland, Wales, inside, outside turn around and out." At which point you would hop out of the elastic to let a friend take their turn!

The kids today would assume we were on another planet. Hell maybe we were, in Planet Poor! Forty forty was a hide and seek game where you would have to make it back to "home", normally a post or part of a wall, before the person on seek would spot you and say, "Forty forty, I see Mary" - at which point, you were busted.

But the most memorable game of all had to be Knock Down Ginger. It was the thrill of running away after you had banged on someone's door and they answer it to nobody.

Mr Invisible. I still chuckle now. We got chased a few times by a Boo Radley lookalike that lived a bit further up the road. Oh how my heartbeat went so fast as we ran for our lives. The older kids would hang out around the corner, aged eleven and twelve they were learning how to smoke cigarettes they had stolen from their parents. Puffing away like dragons but careful to be out of their parents visual range. On occasions a Grandad would comment, "That stuff will stunt your growth" to which they would reply, "Ah, piss off mister".

It was when we lived there that I first started to steal things. Just small personal things - sweeties, badges, lollies, whatever I could fit up my sleeves or inside my small pockets. My parents were good friends with the Fuller family, their Mum was called Anita, the Dad, Alan, and they had two small boys, Kevin and Steven. I was good friends with Kevin. He and I were muckers together and used to get up to all sorts of pranks. We loved to go to the railway line where it joined King Henry's Road and play Chicken which meant running backwards and forwards across the train tracks before the trains came through.

Anita used to tell the most amazing stories about a teddy bear that lived in the forest and I adored listening to them so much that whenever she visited I would plead, "Please

Aunty Anita, tell us a story." I even recited the same stories to my daughter Paris when she was little. She should have written children's books because she was very talented.

But one day, I was eight or nine years old, I couldn't remember what I had done but I was grounded and sulking around the house. It was a pretty ordinary afternoon and fairly peaceful in our house, a miracle really bearing in mind how many children lived there, and then all of a sudden I remember it was mayhem.

Anita was in the street screaming, I can only describe it as a wailing sound. She sobbed and screamed hysterically. Mum rushed out to see what the problem was and told us children to stay indoors while Dad tried to keep us all calm. I ran upstairs and peered through the window. Anita had Kevin in her arms but he wasn't moving and she was unconsolable. My Mum started crying too. Although I was way too young to grasp any concept of the situation, I began to cry because Mum was crying. I knew something was terribly wrong.

Kevin had been electrocuted playing Chicken on the railway line and died pretty much straight away. I couldn't imagine how Anita was feeling. To lose a child must be the worst pain ever and needless to say Anita never fully recovered. Years after, the family emigrated to

Australia for a fresh start, but sadly they lost their other son Steven in a car accident. How do you ever recover from that?

Mum told me years later that at the very moment Kevin was electrocuted, Anita was sitting in her armchair when his picture flew off the wall above the fire place and the lights began to flicker. She knew instantly that Kevin was in trouble, she was a very spiritual lady. When I was told that Kevin had died, I went into shock but I never spoke of him again, until now. I missed him badly, I loved him like a brother.

Shortly afterwards, we moved to Potters Grove and the ninth baby was born, the last of the clan, Michael. Potters Grove was pretty similar to Porchester Road in that again there were poor families together. Someone turned the P into an R on our road sign so it read Rotter's Grove - they weren't wrong!

Our neighbours were the Boyce family, which was a bit weird because, like us, they used to live in Porchester Road but a few doors along. Now they were next door. They consisted of many brothers and sisters but the main attraction was Stewart. He was huge, when I say huge I mean very big for his age. He also had a hunchback and was a bit mentally challenged. I wasn't sure if it was because he knew he was a lot bigger than the other children or whether he knew he was different, but he chose to be extremely cruel to all the children and made whips so he could beat us all. When you went out to play, you'd pray he wasn't around and then on some days, when you thought you were safe and walked two yards from the safety of your house, he would appear from nowhere. Fuck knows how he could hide, he was massive lump.

One day, my Dad had enough of the bully and ordered me to go out and batter Stewart. I was a bit apprehensive but once I got out there and my adrenalin kicked in, I punched him silly with everyone watching. He never bullied anyone ever again, it was the best feeling in the world. My Dad didn't particularly like Stewart because everytime he left the house, he would ask Dad, "Where ya goin' Mr T? Tommy's got a girlfriend." He probably didn't realise he was hitting the nail on the head.

Their backdoor backed onto ours. Like everyone in those days, we always left the doors open and rarely used the front door. One day, my brother Scott saw a tub of ice cream on Stewart's table so he sneaked in there and stole a huge scoop only to find out it was in fact margarine. He nearly vomited because he had eaten an extra-large scoop. Stewart broke his leg pretending to be superman one afternoon jumping off the shed. His sister Jackie was no looker, she had green teeth but fancied the pants of my brother Patrick and used to flash at him from her bedroom window. Boy did we tease him about that. It was a bit like the munster family but the parents were nice people, just fucking scary in the dark.

Another smelly family in the street were the Murrays. Mum was good friends with Mrs Murray. I felt sorry for the daughter Sandra because of their poverty situation, so one day I stole a load of clothes for her so she was all dressed up, and what a transformation.

Our neighbours on the other side were Timmy Jones and his single Mum - there was no Dad around. She was a sweet old lady with her long hair pulled up into a bun and had very sharp features like the witch on the Wizard of Oz. I used to run errands to the shops for her on a daily basis and she would give me a bit of small change. I didn't like to go in her house because it was very dark and dreary, kind of creepy. Timmy was a bit like that too. He was tall, big built with very dark hair, about thirty three years old and a violent drunk. I felt sorry for his poor Mum who had to put up with him when he began his drunken screaming fits. All of the kids were scared of him, including me.

One day, Timmy was in his garden talking to my sister Tracy through the fence when all of a sudden he whipped out his trouser snake and stuck it through the wire fence. Tracy screamed and ran in distraught to tell Mum what had happened. Mum called the police. I couldn't stop laughing and thought the whole episode was hilarious. The police arrived and all they kept asking Tracy was, how big was his willy? My Dad went ballistic and I was no longer allowed to run errands for Mrs Jones. I did anyway without their knowledge. Timmy must have been sent to a hospital or something because we never saw him again. He must have disappeared, or Dad killed him and buried him in the back garden. I wouldn't put it past him.

I developed an obsession with money from an early age. Dad would sometimes give me a few coins - maybe fifty pence or twenty five pence which in 1970 could buy you shit loads of sweets. I kept nagging my Dad to buy me a second hand bicycle and when he finally got me one, I was ecstatic and turned it into a money making scheme. I hired it out to the other children less fortunate than me, though not by the hour as these days you can do in Dulwich Park. My bicycle was in demand, for just twenty five pence or fifty pence per ride, it all depended on the person as to how much I charged, I was quite the little entrepreneur. I also ran errands for a few elderly ladies that lived further along the road, anything to make a few extra bucks. I used my sweet little face to my advantage, asking for jobs with a cute smile that they couldn't refuse. I had the bare cheek to ask.

Our milkman played a big part in my childhood too. He used to deliver everything - eggs, bacon, sausages, butter, orange juice, tea, coffee; it was like he was a regular, walking, talking little minimart. Mum usually paid him in milk tokens and had a permanent outstanding bill. We children devised a plan whereby one of us would distract the milkman so the others could run out the backdoor and help ourselves to the goods on his van. Mum never noticed because she was usually distracted with the smaller children or Dad. The one thing I loved about the milkman was his broken biscuits, who on earth would invented that? Selling broken biscuits? I'm sure I'm not alone on this one, but it wasn't until I reached puberty that I discovered whole biscuits, I was gobsmacked and in heaven.

While our milkman produced the goods, the dustmen were a load of rubbish and seemed scarce. I wasn't unsure if there was some sort of dispute or strike going on at the time but I remember our garden was permanently littered. This escalated further when I was in the garden one day. Somehow, I managed to stand on a rusty nail that shot straight through my big toe.

Initially I was unaware of the nail protruding through my toe and tried shaking off the plank of wood that seemed stuck to my foot. The next thing I knew, Mum had me in a pushchair walking me to the emergency room at the hospital. I had a fear of needles and had to be restrained by three or four nurses, all astounded by how such a little delicate child had so much inner strength. I became The Incredible Hulk! This inner strength has always been with me and remains with me today. Yet, despite the injection ordeal, it was all worth it in the end because Dad gave me lots of cuddles and a couple of Curly Wurlys.

Sylvia and I had one year between us in age and we often got mistaken for twin sisters. Both of us were pretty with long hair but that was soon short lived. The dreaded nits came to town, not just to our town but our household. The sudden outbreak of headlice drove my Mum so insane, she gave us all homemade haircuts. Sylvia and I soon looked like we had escaped from a mental hospital. Huge chunks had disappeared from our fringes and the rest was as though she had stuck a bowl on our heads and cut round it. We all know that children can be cruel and these new hairstyles caused us to be ridiculed by others our age. It didn't particularly bother me but Sylvia was mortified. The fact that they were harassing and clearly upsetting a member of my family filled me with such a rage that I punched a few of them until they apologised. I became the Nightmare on Elm Street – well - Nightmare on Potter's Grove!

Nobody fucked with any member of my family.

It was during this phase of the dodgy Beatles style haircuts that I began to dress like a Tom Boy. No more girlie dresses. Just t-shirts, jeans and Dr Martens boots from now on. I refused point blank to wear dresses. I am still a bit of a Tom Boy now, but with a girlie touch. Mum couldn't afford to buy me an entire new wardrobe so I began to steal clothes.

When I was a teenager I used to adore Marc Bolan and T Rex. I adored all the songs from the Telegram Sam album, and would continuously play the records. The record player was more like a suitcase - you had to virtually put your entire head inside just to put the record on. It closed like a suitcase too, with two clips each side and three speeds; thirty three, forty five and seventy eight. Single records were placed on the forty five setting, LPs thirty three and fuck knows what the seventy eight was for apart from when you were playing a record, you'd turned it to seventy eight for it to sound like the singers were on helium. That would send us into fits of giggles.

You kids today with your MP3s and iPods have no idea of the struggle! The trick with the old fashioned record player was that if you had a favourite song, you only had to lift up the arm and push it back so it repeatedly played once it had finished, this drove my Dad mad. One day when I was repeatedly playing Gladys Knight and The Pips' 'Baby don't change your mind', my Dad flew into a rage and smashed up my record, shouting and screaming like Rumple Stiltskin. Ironic really because he repeated himself daily trying to brainwash us all with his tips on life.

"Never trust ANYONE," Dad would say. "Never be a Grass." They were endless.

My old best friend and I at the time went shopping to Littlewoods in Kingston. If she is reading this, she may well recall this day, it is still pretty vivid to me. We stole some new jeans, and they weren't just ordinary jeans, these had lions on the front pockets, how cool was that! I had such a buzz that we had got away with it - that we both returned to steal more clothes, shoes, underwear - everything. We basically rigged ourselves with complete new wardrobes. I gave my Mum a bullshit story that a friend's parents were loaded and had taken me shopping. She appeared to believe me but she was so preoccupied with all the other children, she probably had no time to think about it. Raising nine children leaves little time to ponder about things. Mum seemed happy about the story, but I couldn't let it lie and one day, when I didn't want to go to school, I confessed to my Mum. She didn't react quite as I imagined. There was no screaming or shouting, just calm and said, "Kim, I'm deeply shocked but glad that you have told me the truth."

I then realised that I could probably confide in my Mum about anything. Mum tried her best to stop me but I wasn't listening to anybody and over the years, she accepted my path. If I chose to shoplift then I would suffer the consequences.

A few years later, when I came home loaded with stolen goods, Mum had a premonition. "Quick Kim, I think the police are coming, get the stuff," she said.

"Where are we going Mum?"

"Just do as yer told for once Kim."

So I followed her outside and she proceeded to hang all the stolen clothes I had for sale on the washing line.

"There's no one coming Mum, stop being paranoid."

But I went along with her plan and helped her hang the clothes out just to humour her. Sure enough, not long after, the police arrived to search the house and they found nothing because it was all hanging on the washing line. Thank God for Mums, eh!

My Mum, Susannah Browne, was a very slim, petite lady with blonde highlighted hair, small features, olive skin and big brown eyes. She came from a respectable family having spent her childhood riding ponies and winning gymkhana rosettes. Her mother was an alcoholic and I don't think she had an easy childhood. For a lady that had given birth naturally to nine children, she had a figure to die for and not one stretch mark. She never drank - her only vice was cigarettes but practically played the solo parent as Dad was neither a great husband nor father in many ways.

Dad liked to gamble, party and charm the ladies - a regular play boy, but nevertheless he was still my hero. He taught me many things like family values and manners. In hindsight, he was a bit of an arsehole as a husband. He wasn't the financial provider for the family and barely at home, so all the responsible things were left to Mum to resolve. She would order our Christmas presents out of the Littlewoods catalogue, and spent the rest of the year paying it off. Otherwise we would have had nothing.

With my parents the way they were, it made me even more rebellious and cheeky. Clowning about was my way of life. It brightened up my days and I loved to see people laugh, well

I still do. I would play tricks on people, hide and jump out to startle them. I adored my family and have many fond memories of a happy childhood. I loved to entertain and at night would sing opera, hanging out of my bedroom window to entertain the street. "Gooooooood nigghhhhhhht" I would sing.

I slept walked too, and many a night Dad would catch me out of bed walking up the road in my pyjamas like Wee Willy Winkle. He never woke me, just turned me around so I would walk back home. Convulsions were another common thing at home. As our fevers rose, we would have convulsions. I guess Calpol hadn't really hit the streets back then. I recall witnessing my brother Lee having 'a fit' one night. Mum would scream for me to fetch a spoon then jam the spoon inside his mouth to prevent him from swallowing his tongue. I hated seeing Lee in this way. It upset me to tears. I mothered him and took him everywhere with me, I loved him so, so much. As a small boy, he was very sickly and suffered from a bowel disorder which the doctors neglected and it ruined some of his childhood.

Food shopping with Mum was an ordeal in itself. I don't know how she did it. Picture this - three or four kids in the pram, others hanging off it, I used to walk behind waiting for Lee to walk into a lamp post as he generally did. He was a clumsy boy. He'd then start screaming and Mum would get distracted from her shopping to try and console him. The food we bought would be stuffed under the pram and it used to collapse nearly every time, so we children would be running around collecting all the food that was rolling away. This was not a one off occurrence - it used to happen frequently. How the hell did Mum cope? She just took it all in her stride, as calm as ever. I guess that was normal to her, not a care in the world.

Mind you, Mum did smoke heavily, about sixty cigarettes a day. She bought ten No.10s, or Park Drive and she always had a ciggy on the go. I don't remember her eating a lot. She had a sweet tooth and bought herself the occasional treat, chocolate; Fry's Chocolate Creams, Toblerones and Crunchie bars. I'm the same but minus the cigarettes - it was the cigarettes that eventually took their toll on poor Mum. She developed emphysema and died aged fifty two. She was so, so young. She never had it easy over the years raising nine children on a shoestring but she did the best she could and she loved every one of us.

Dad would never take us all out as a family. He would say there's too many of us and "it's embarrassing". He was ashamed that we were a large family, though the real truth was that he used that as an excuse so he could go off and do what he wanted like going to the betting shop, play snooker and cards, down the pub with his mates, or charming some pretty barmaid with his funny anecdotes. He sometimes took a few of us to the snooker hall in Kingston. Sylvia and I loved it because his friends would make a fuss over us, give us money, saying, "Ay Tommy, these girls will break some 'earts one day, eh?"

Boy, they weren't wrong. We broke hearts and caused mayhem at the same time, more than once! As the eldest, my Dad taught me that blood is thicker than water. He would say in his gruff tone, "You kids stick together and protect each ovva". I took what he said as the bible and lived my life based on those words.

As I was the eldest, it was my job to protect all my siblings. They were my responsibility. I became the street's Rocky Balboa, nobody messed with my brothers and sisters or they had me to deal with. I also discovered that I didn't seem to have a sense of fear, nobody scared me. It didn't matter how big or how small they were I would fight to the death and always won. I became invincible. Sometimes my protection would get out of hand as I ended up going to prison for it.

My sister Sylvia was a bit of an enigma. As we grew older she became an inverted snob and loathed the fact that we were poor. We all used to invite our friends round to our house, all except Sylvia because she was clearly ashamed of her background. She would pretend that she lived at a different address and yearned to be posh. Yes, we weren't living in The Ritz - it was rough and ready, but was still home.

It came to the point that we were so not posh, were all pretty excited to receive new - well second hand - double beds. What the people who had either sold, or donated, them to us neglected to say was the fact that these beds had hidden extras. Yes you guessed it - they arrived infested with bed bugs. Little tiny blacky brownish things that darted about faster than Speedy Gonzalez. They had crunchy bodies so you had to pop them to death. With up to four of us in one bed that was uncomfortable enough but then the invasion of the bugs, yuck! I began to sleep on the floor, outside, bug free which sounded a better thought.

I remember being the child with the smelly house. Everything smelt including us children, but it wasn't our fault. Other children were cruel and would say "You smell", but because this person was me, I became immune to the smell. It didn't bother me what people said, but my siblings would get offended and I would end up fighting to defend their honour.

It's probably why I'm a clean freak now. My OCD stems from never wanting to return to being the smelly kid. Whenever I would visit a friend's house and it smelt fresh and cosy, it was a nice feeling and I knew in my heart that one day I would have a home like that.

Unlike Sylvia, I never felt ashamed of my home and would bring all my friends to the house. People took me as you found me, and generally my friends never returned - only kidding. A lot of them were from similar backgrounds to me. Others were intrigued to think so many of us lived in that one house, and with so little.

When I visited houses of my friends, I would sometimes be in awe of very simple things. The beauty of their home would absorb my mind and I would think "Wow, I'd love a bedroom like this".

There was a children's programme that I used to watch called Attic, about a poor young girl that lived in the loft and a magic wizard transformed her room from a dreary one to a beautiful one, fit for a princess. I imagined I was the girl in the show and dreamed a wizard would transform our house. Oh to dream! We never possessed material things, but what we had was a sense of family values and a sense of humour, you could never survive without the latter. There was noise, always noise, normally laughter, sometimes tears and big arguments - but that's children for you.

At one stage, Mum began her own life of crime through desperation. She and a friend used to go shopping every Tuesday. I knew what she was up to, it was pretty obvious. Each week, she would arrive home with new clothes for all of us. One day I counted up the total of all the price tags on the underwear and knew it amounted to much more than Mum had in her purse. I never revealed her dark secret, I kept it to myself. But her criminal career was short lived because "Bonnie and Bonnie" got caught, perhaps by the knicker police, but she then gave up her life of crime and the new clothes stopped coming.

Every Sunday, Mum would take us to Richmond Park for a picnic, albeit the weather was alright and it wasn't raining. We would be extremely excited and loved the park. I used to pick the biggest tree and climb it as high as I could go. It gave me a sense of escape and power. It was so peaceful up there and I could see for miles. Going up the tree was easy but getting down was another story. Mum would lose her temper, probably because I was deaf and I couldn't hear her worried cries of "Get down from there NOW."

"Kim, the fire brigade are on their way," she would add.

The park was like a sanctuary in those days, apart from the odd flasher who, for some strange reason, always wore a long brown mac coat. It was pretty safe for children to play, not dangerous like today. Our generation definitely had the best childhoods, the freedom. Children can no longer play out for fear of sexual predator's preying on them like a lioness hunting her dinner, it seems so unfair.

As you can imagine my Mum didn't really have much free time for herself or a social life. However, occasionally, she would go off to a Tupperware or Avon party. I would be left in charge of my siblings. I had to keep them entertained or they would end up arguing amongst themselves and at that point I was getting fed up of being forever in fights, defending them.

One night, I devised a fighting game to toughen them up. My plan was that I was their trainer and got them to fight each other, one-on-one. Let the battles commence. First up was Patrick v Sylvia, which was funny. As they scuffled with each other, Sylvia's skirt managed to fall down exposing her rather gigantic Alice in Wonderland knickers. Patrick's friend Rodney was there so she felt extremely humiliated probably because we all roared with laughter at the sight of those knickers. We were traumatised!

The winner got to enter round two with a new opponent, this was Patrick v Lee. Lee went ballistic because he was always a sore loser and gave it all he had and more. But the sight of Lee losing the plot just made Patrick start to laugh uncontrollably. His laughter was infectious and so we all began to giggle hysterically, so I had to throw in the towel and cancel the match.

My shoe fetish must stem back to my childhood memories of winter time. Mum throwing anything on the fire to keep warm as there wasn't any money for coal, we used to joke about it but she actually did burn some of my shoes, probably because I had started stealing by then and had more than the others. Not only was I stealing shoes (C & A left them out in pairs) but I also liked rummaging through the jumble sales - I liked hats and shoes.

When doing this, I'd use to sing, "Let's all go to Tesco's, where Sylvia gets her best clothes. Kimmy can't grumble, cos hers come from the jumble."

Another thing Mum did was look to see if any of my clothes had a Marks & Spencer label inside. If they did, she would take them back and get a full refund.

What is it with women and shoes? I had an obsession with them. At one point I owned hundreds of pairs. I was also addicted to owning basic toiletries, and even today have the bathroom with new spare toothbrushes, just in case someone spends the night at my home unexpectedly. They do not have to suffer the humiliation of cleaning their teeth with their finger.

Holidays as you could imagine were not exactly priority on my Mum's list as we never had any money to spare. So we were all elated one year when social services paid for us all to stay at a caravan site in Selsey Bay. We were going on holiday, yes all of us! This was better than Christmas and any birthday. An entire week in a holiday park by the sea, yippee! It was one of the best weeks ever. I wore a dress similar to one Twiggy and Cilla Black were modelling at the time. Our hair was short and still a bit fucked up from the headlice haircut but that no longer seemed to matter as far as we were concerned. We had won the fucking lottery, I felt. It was so cool, beach bums during the day and to the social club to dance away in the nights. Each night there was a new competition and one night I was picked to help judge The Knobbly Knees contest. I gave first prize to Albert, the only Down Syndrome boy there, he was bowled over.

I was so pleased that he was so happy and afterwards danced with him. I could see from his face that he was so happy and that made me feel happy too. Obviously I became the centre of my family who took the piss out of me because I was dancing with a "different" boy but I didn't care about that. Seeing Albert smile and having fun pleased me.

That night, we returned to the caravan giggling like the over-excited children we were. Come to think of it, that caravan felt like a Tardis inside to fit all of us, there were bodies everywhere. As we calmed down, there was a heavy knock on the door - we all shat ourselves. "It's yer boyfriend, Albert," my brothers all joked. It wasn't Albert, but his mother. She came to thank me for making Albert's night. She explained that he had a fantastic evening and I made his holiday special because before then, most of the other children avoided him. Probably the reason being they didn't know how to react around him. What she didn't know was that it had also made my night pretty special too, just knowing I had brought joy to Albert – it brought me joy. I gave the others a smug look and slept pretty well that night, doing good deeds for others brings good upon yourself. I truly believe that.

Like many young girls, I was a dreamer and one of my dreams was to become an actress. It never materialised to anything. I did attend some drama classes in New Malden and the teacher said I was gifted, but Mum couldn't afford to keep paying for the classes so I had to cease going. But seriously, aren't we all actors in our own lives? Don't we act like one person indoors and another one when we are amongst colleagues and friends? Throughout my shoplifting career I have been many different people in various disguises. I was Mrs Doubtfire and even dressed as a young boy once.

I didn't particularly enjoy school and frequently skipped classes. One day I knew Mum had arranged to go somewhere and wouldn't be home, so after the coast was clear, I doubled back to the house. I spent hours cleaning the entire downstairs. I dusted and polished, swept the floor then washed anything else that looked grubby. I was a proper Cinderella. Once I had completed my task of transforming the house, I sat down to bask in my glory. I could not believe the changes I made and how fresh everything smelt. It felt so good and the house even seemed cosier. The cooking, washing and ironing alone took up all my Mum's time. I soon shat my pants though when I heard Mum arrive home.

"What have you done, and why aren't you at school?" she shouted.

She'd continued to rant for a further ten minutes then looked around, gave me a wry smile and said, "It sure smells nice and fresh in here, thank you."

She knew I was only trying to help. I loved to iron too. I'd spend the entire Sunday just ironing all our clothes, bin liners full. I know there are many people reading this thinking how can anyone like ironing, but I did and still do. It's therapeutic.

Moving into my shoplifting memories now - as I said earlier, I started off stealing small things. Kids' stuff, sweeties, badges - things that fitted up my sleeve. I then decided, as I was sick of there being no goodies in the larder, to begin stealing food for the house. I got away with it so easily because of my angelic looks, but little did the shop assistants realise that the sweet innocent girl buying just a few groceries for her Mum had three bags more of goodies stuffed away in her trolley, all stolen. That gave me such a buzz.

By this point, I was around thirteen years old. My brainy friend from Tiffin Girls School decided to come with me to Barkers of Kensington where I stole a childs suit worth thirty eight pounds. That was a lot of money for us girls. I just couldn't resist the temptation. It seemed too easy to do, so I stole a few more. We waited a few hours then my friend returned two of the suits and they gave her a full refund there and then. A little while later I returned the other two, again receiving a full refund. What a roll we were on! We were loaded, one hundred and fifty two pounds gained in a matter of hours. We felt like royalty and decided to hit the denim shops for F.U.S jeans. We robbed so many pairs, we had to spread the remainders around the shelves so they didn't look empty. A few more shops to rob after that, then we hailed a black taxi for home, heavily laden with stolen property and buzzing that we hadn't got caught.

We next found an unoccupied boat moored on the River Thames in Kingston. We broke into it and squatted on it for weeks. It was Aladdin's cave, stuffed with all our ill-gotten gains because we started going crazy on a mammoth shoplifting spree. It later bit us on the backside though. The owners of the boat returned and we were arrested. All our treasures were confiscated.

I would not reveal anything to the police about how we acquired the goods, but my so-called best friend sang like Tweety Pie and told them everything - times, dates, the names of the shops we robbed. I really didn't know how she remembered it all! That was the end of that friendship. So much for Tiffin Girls School with no loyalty. We were only kids. I guess she got scared, but I wished she said nothing. I was so popular in those days, I couldn't imagine why...

Being the eldest, I was "The Boss", as Dad would say, "Always look out for your family, you only get one." As a teenager, this meant I was involved in a lot of fights, usually defending a sibling or friend. I developed a reputation to be feared and this resulted in many appointments to Kingston Police Station. I gained a record for violence, but hell - when you are that young, you'd never think of the repercussions later in your life. It also meant that I earned an appointment with a psychiatrist.

"Kim, what would you like to do when you grow older?" my psychiatrist asked me.

"Be a 'airdresser," I replied.

"Well, I'm not too sure about such a violent girl as yourself being in charge of a pair of scissors, don't you think?"

Mum, who was there when he said that, was absolutely fuming. If looks could kill, he would have been dead on the spot. "How dare you!" She said. "If anyone needs to see a doctor it's you, you twisted little man. Kim get yer coat on, we´re leaving"

She shouted as she marched me out of the door. I'm pretty sure the whole waiting room heard her. "Bloody cheek, who does he think he is? C'mon we're going home," she'd add.

From the age of nine to sixteen, I was just learning to shoplift, mainly in Kingston's Town Centre. We hung around in a big gang and robbed the shops, usually pulling a granny style shopping trolley to load the goods into. They were deep and held more than one bag. We would hit all the shops, then afterwards go out and get drunk. One day, we decided to go further afield and had a day trip shopping in Hounslow. This turned out to be a bad idea because at the end of our day's hoisting, the police surrounded us at the final shop, and we all got arrested.

At fifteen years old, I discovered alcohol. Because I was making money, I used to buy rum and coke for us all - our gang - plus cider. We would drink more or less on a daily basis. Once, we were walking through Kingston; Bev, Johnny, Sylvia, myself and a few others became involved in a fight with a group of students. Bev had initiated it because she was so drunk. Afterwards, Bev and I were in the middle of a scuffle and somebody called the police. We both spent the night in Kingston Police cells sobering up. Tragically many from our crowd turned to drugs later in life and have since passed. Not all bad news, however. Others went straight, obtaining normal jobs and raising families of their own. I seemed to be the only one unable to stop stealing!

By then I also got my first professional tattoo. I say 'professional' because when I was fifteen, I bought some Indian ink from Books, Bits and Bobs in Kingston and did a home jobby. I did it at home with a needle and wrote Kim + Terry on my left wrist. It seemed a good idea at the time while my brother Scott watched me. Terry and I were best friends. Scott wanted one too but didn't like the pain so I cut his arm and just poured the ink on it, poor boy. For the professional job, I had a butterfly with the word Mum underneath. I figured that if I had her name on it, she was less likely to scream at me for having a tattoo. Sure enough, she was more lenient. I could tell she didn't like it but she accepted it. Too late, I could hardly wash it off. I wasn't worried about the wrath of my Dad at the time because he wasn't at home. He seemed to never come home.

Although Dad was smart, funny and handsome, he could also be pretty scary when he lost his temper. Everyone dived for cover - a real scary bastard and he'd put the fear of God in many of us children. He had an obsession with golf, and practically every other sport you could think of. Golf was about the only one he played, apart from snooker, if you count that as a sport! Each morning, he would leave early about 6am, to walk to Coombe Hill golfcourse and would caddy for the rich men and many famous. He introduced my brother Scott to his world, plus gambling which wasn't too clever.

Dad had his favourites. I was number one, followed by Patrick and Scott. Obviously he loved all of his kids, but he would go out of his way for us three. When he finally left home to move in with his girlfriend, I didn't think it would affect me. As I write this book, I realise clearly it did, more than I realised. I used to deliberately get arrested so Mum would call Dad in a crisis, as she did, and then I got to see him. I managed to get detained three times in one week!

The other trick I did to gain Dad's attention was to run away from home. This worked too, but he never stayed longer than one night. He never had a shortage of girlfriends, and his nasty side would prevail. This was usually indoors though, rarely in public. I knew he was far from perfect but to me he was, if that makes any sense. I adored him and let his bad side slide. I think I've also managed to get his sense of humour - one of his qualities.

Back to my teenage years, I had many haunts I liked to go to. The Coronation Halls in

Kingston and Surbiton Assembly rooms were my favourites. We would put on our gladrags, Lionel Blair's, flares and boogie the night away, young and carefree. The fashion was pretty bizarre when I look back but even nowadays it still is in ways. It seems trends return but with a slightly new angle to them - different patterns and colours, pretty boring really.

I had a Saturday job at the local picture house – that's cinema to you young people! I was paid to dance on stage and when the intermission came on, I became one of the ice cream sellers. I remember feeling really proud when I won the belly dancing competition. Fuck it, I couldn't do that now - damn middle age! I loved to dance and also loved to be the centre of attention. Following my proud moment as the belly dancer queen, I took it upon myself to convince a friend to partner up with me and enter The Assembly Rooms rock 'n' roll competition. Yay, we won that too. I'm chuckling to myself because, as I write this, I can still remember our dance moves all those years ago. I must have had a bit of Elvis the Pelvis in me or Michael Jackson.

I walked everywhere too. I loved walking. Just as well because not many people owned cars back then. Dad used to take me to visit his Mum, Nanny Bridget or Bridget the midget, as I sometimes called her. She was just over four feet high, a Mrs Pepperpot. Every Sunday he would walk from New Malden to Ewell Road, Surbiton where she lived, above a piano shop. It was a fair trot and took us quite a while to get there. I loved going. I adored Nanny Bridget and the stories she used to tell me - some funny, others sad. She and her husband had emigrated from Northern Ireland yet she still spoke with a thick Irish accent. She loved to sing a few songs too, thank fuck I was deaf as she was no Mariah Carey. She was a funny old lady, a lot like the Nan in the Catherine Tate sketches. I used to visit her often and once older, would go alone without Dad.

Nanny Bridget would send me to do her shopping. Nothing was easy. The bread had to be from the Bakers, butter from another shop, meat from another, the list was endless with instructions. God forbid if you went into Sainsbury's and bought it all together. I'd steal the meat on her shopping list, she knew too. Little did I know, I went with her to Key market's supermarket once, she used to swap the price tickets and pocket Oxo cubes.

She loved apple and rhubarb crumble with custard and cooked amazing food. I loved her dearly. One day, during one of my many visits, she received a phone call from a lawyer trying to locate the whereabouts of my Mum. It transpired that Mum had been left some money in a will from a long lost relative. She was the only living beneficiary. Mum and I had drifted apart by then but I made sure I relayed the message to her.

When my parents split during my teens, Dad officially moved in with his girlfriend Maggie and her three children. Patrick and I were forever in trouble with the police (he liked to steal cars, go joyriding and being chased by the police, like in the Dukes of Hazzard, that was his buzz), so Mum decided she needed a fresh start with the other children and arranged for a council estate swap to a house in Basingstoke. I had left home by then and spent more time visiting my Dad than her as I moved into a flat on the Cambridge Estate. He lived there too and he looked out for me during my troubled times.

It was a case of Mum being out of sight and out of mind. Whenever I went to visit her, there was always some dramas going on between the children and because I had done so my entire life, I would get involved and make things worse. Now, the others no longer looked at me as "The Boss". I was never around so my opinion wasn't valued. We'd all row which would escalate so it became best that I stayed away.

These frictions would escalate so much, it felt as though when I called Mum to say I'm coming to visit, it never seemed convenient. I could never get my head around the fact that I had to make an appointment to see my own mother. That wasn't right, so I stopped calling. Mum was not very house proud when we grew up but as soon as she moved to Basingstoke she changed. The house was spotless and she began taking more care of her personal appearance. I guess she was depressed before but her new home brought her happiness. Depression is a terrible illness, I've been dealt my fair share over the years, but I always managed to bounce back and refused to let in linger, fuck that! I have found my strength and a passion for being happy, because if you are unhappy, you have nothing.

Talking of which, yippee, I have just won twenty five pounds on the lottery, my luck is in!

In the early years, while I was still trying to master the art of shoplifting, I recruited mainly family members. I used to joke we had a family business. Since Mum moved away, one-by-one, my brothers and sisters began to visit me - usually during the school holidays. Patrick, Sylvia and I remained in Kingston but the others went to Basingstoke. Every time one would arrive, I'd take them shopping with me and steal an entire new wardrobe-worth to go home with, and gifts for my Mum. I took them with me and tried to teach them how to shoplift, not very clever now as I write this, but as a young girl I thought I was educating them on how to survive. It was the only way I knew how to live, and I found that I liked doing it.

At the age of fifteen, I paid a shop assistant, who worked at a menswear shop in Kingston, to turn a blind eye so I could steal. The only problem with that was that I became so greedy and took nearly everything, that they ended up going out of business and closing down. In my teenage years, I had teamed up with a friend called Maxine. We worked well together. We were the dream team and had daily hoists. You name it, we could get you it - and there were no shortage of customers.

There were times we'd nearly get caught. One day, when my son Damon was a toddler in the pushchair, we stuffed a load of leather jackets under his pushchair. Well fuck me, we nearly died on the way out of the shop - he began pulling the jackets out in plain sight of everyone. Luckily, not one member of staff noticed and we got away with it, but I never took any children shoplifting with me ever again after that.

We used to enter the stockroom at Hennes in Kingston (now called H&M) with big black binliners and stuff them with clothes. Maxine and I worked well together, others helped too. We established a team, and this was way before the voucher system (which I'll explain later in the book).

In the early 1980s, we had our own "fence", Ray. He drove up daily to Kingston from Bognor Regis, took all the stolen goods, then paid me on Friday. This went on for a few years. I was addicted to the feeling of getting away with it. It was already my drug of choice but I never realised it. It was all about precise timing and I am a great believer in "The early bird gets the worm". That's me, the early bird – well, a thieving magpie more like!

Our gang one day decided to steal from Miss Selfridge. In those days, the alarms were just paper and easily pulled off. I cleared the entire rail and just as we were leaving the alarm went off. I had accidently forgotten to remove one of the alarms. Everyone started to run down the alleyway alongside the shop and when the young assistant came out into the street I jumped out in front of her saying "What's wrong, what 'appened?" She had no idea I was with the thieves and by the time she had explained what was happening they had all got away. Ali Baba and the forty thieves were long gone.

I was arrested far too many times as a teenager. I didn't care as I was still trying to master my chosen trade. I resigned myself to the fact that, because I had a criminal record as a convicted shoplifter, I faced difficulties finding employment. There was no other path to follow. I needed to perfect my game and turn it into a lucrative business. No matter what, I had to teach myself, learn to be one of the best ever shoplifters.

I felt that I needed to give you an idea of my early days and childhood so to explain how I became me. By explaining my past, it would help give you a better perspective as to who I am today. You all know me as "Britain's Shameless Shoplifter", but that is just a part of me - or should I say *was* a part of me, a huge part in fact. I am also Kim Farry. A human being, a daughter, someone's sister, someone's aunt, a mother and now someone's grandmother.

Chapter 2 - Short Sharp Shock

When I was sixteen, Mum went to see the local clairvoyant, Mrs Young. She was an elderly lady who held a piece of your jewellery in order to proceed in telling you your fortune. I was sceptical at the time, although it was said that she sometimes helped the police on some of their cases. She said to Mum, "Send me your eldest daughter, I need to see her. And don't worry about the payment dear."

So off I trotted to pay the lady a visit. Dad was against anything like that. He hated it all, Tarot cards the lot. He used to shout, "If she's that fuckin' good, why don't she ever win at Bingo? You're wasting yer money." There I was a few days later seated in front of Mrs Young.

"My dear, you are going to prison on the seventeenth, but I can't make out which month. That's not coming through clearly but the number seventeen is," she said.

I froze. Dad was right - there was no way I was going to prison, and I only had minor offences on my current juvenile record. I believed she was talking bollocks, until she continued.

"And that ring you're wearing my luv, you stole it from a poor old lady and she's pretty heartbroken cos it's got sentimental value. She wants it back."

Shit, fuck. Now I thought Dad's wrong, how the fuck did she know that? A bunch of us scallywags had been in the lady's house and I did take the ring.

Mrs Young finished with, "And while yer at it, clean yer Mother's back garden. It's a blooming disgrace, rubbish everywhere!"

I left there red faced with shame knowing I had taken the ring from a heartbroken lady, and immediately returned it to her. Mrs Young had magic powers and I was unnerved by the whole experience. The following day, I cleared the back garden. There was at least thirty giant binliners full of rubbish.

A few months later I had a court appearance which fell on the seventeenth of November. I was so convinced I was going home that day. I had even forgotten the episode with Mrs Young. The time came for Judge Gilby to speak.

"Stand up young lady," he said. "Can you honestly tell me that you are going to change your ways?"

I rose to my feet then answered "Yes Judge" in a clear and positive voice.

"So do I," he continued. "But after six months to two years Borstal Training." And that was that. It took me a few seconds to realise what had actually happened then terror and panic set in. Some friends of mine were upstairs watching the events in the gallery. I jumped the dock and tried to run free, screaming hysterically but was soon apprehended and escorted to the cells below the courtroom.

I was devastated and in shock, plus terrified of what was going to happen to me. To make it even worse, Mum had recently forced me to watch the film "Scrubbers" - about a female Borstal - so I was really shitting it. There was also a weird sense of excitement because I genuinely did not know what I was in for. Both my parents arrived to visit me as I waited to be transported to Holloway Prison.

"Just keep yer 'ead down, stay out a trouble, do yer time an'you'll be 'ome in six monffs," said Dad. This came from the voice of experience because he had himself been behind bars before. But little did he know how much trouble I managed to get in.

On route to Holloway Prison, there were a few of us in a small van that had individual boxes, and we were all allocated one. Why? Fuck know. We were hardly "Silence of the Lamb" material. Once we arrived, it wasn't nearly as bad as I expected. We each had to book in at the reception area. We stated our names, why we were there, were strip searched and then the doctor gave us each a medical. From there, we were given our bedding, night clothes, soap, toothpaste, a toothbrush and a hair comb before finally being taken to make one phone call to our loved ones to let them know we had arrived safely. I looked around me and thought, "There is no fucking way I am staying here."

I was lucky enough to be allocated my own cell rather than share in the dormitory. That suited me just fine. I was just out of my cell to enquire whether I was going to be transferred to another prison when out of the corner of my eye I spotted an inmate wearing my clothes, the cheeky bitch. I confronted her, "What ya doin', that's my clobber?" She just laughed in my face so I reported it to the screw, prison officer. "Don't worry love, she does it all the time, I'll sort it for you," she reassured me. The girl in question was clearly nuts, deranged in my eyes. I thought, "Nah mate I can't be dealing with a crank, I'm the cranky one!"

Holloway Prison was pretty boring and consisted of mainly drug addicts. But after one week, I was shipped out to the open Borstal, East Sutton Park in Maidstone. Once we girls arrived, we had a grand tour of the place. It was a lot nicer than Holloway, a huge open farm. Yet, I didn't care how nice it was. I had it in my head that I was going home, no matter what. Maybe watching the film "Papillon" had affected my brain, but in my head I was saying, "I'm the Boss, nobody can keep me here against my will, not even Her Majesty's Services." So I remained alert and kept my eyes open at all times for any remote possibility of escape.

Nobody supervised the quiet room. It had bars on the windows so you could only open them ajar but I noticed that if you removed the screws above they would fully open. Every half an hour, one prison officer would check on us. So I managed to steal a knife from the kitchen and with two other inmates, we planned our escape. I carefully released the screws from the windows and well before the guard came for his half hourly check on us, we jumped out. We knew we only had half an hour until the alarm would be raised so we had to move fast.

"Fuck, I've 'urt my ankle," said one of the girls. "Me too".

It was a fair drop to the outside ground. "No fuckin' time to moan, let's run girls," I whispered.

Boy, did we run. We managed to make it to the train station which was pretty good going because not one of us knew our way around, but now we hit a snag. None of us had any money and we needed to get on the train. The ticket master was there.

"Shit, what now?"

"Don't worry, I've got a plan." I said boldly.

I then approached the ticket man with tears streaming down my face.

"Whatever is wrong, young lady. There there, there's nothing that bad," he said.

"We all lied to our parents," I sobbed. "Said we were stayin' at each ovvers 'ouse cos we 'ad planned to stay out all night, but we got scared walking the streets and now we wanna go 'ome but spent all our money."

"Now now, calm down young lady, you and yer mates get on the train," he said.

"Really, oh fank you so much," I replied and we all jumped on the train.

How we laughed as the train pulled away! One of my mates said, "And this year's Bafta award goes to..." She hesitated whilst pretending to open an imaginary envelope, "Kim Farry".

We all giggled like overexcited schoolgirls. With the difficult part over, now to get home to Mum's house. We arrived at the door but Mum was far from pleased to see me. She went crazy at me.

"What the hell do you think you are doing? Are you mad Kim? You're a bloody convicted criminal, what have you silly girls done?"

I was devastated. I truly thought Mum would be pleased to see me, "Can't we just stay for Christmas?" I pleaded.

"No you can't. One night Kim and you're going back."

So the next day the police arrived to take us all back to prison. I maintained that the other girls had forced me to run with them and being the smallest, using my sweet demure smile, I think the authorities believed me. The two girls were shipped off to Bullwood Hall, a closed prison but I went back to Holloway for a week then returned to East Sutton Park. I received another two months on top of my sentence for my punishment. Despite the extra two months that didn't seem to deter me, I soon planned another escape. I was Papillon but without the cockroaches and shaking hands with a dry leper.

This time I went with one other girl but we decided to go our separate ways once we were clear from the prison. Mum reacted much the same as the last time. "What the hell is wrong with you?" she shouted.

I didn't get it. I was only a child really, just sixteen. Why wasn't Mum pleased to see me? I couldn't grasp the reality of my actions, nor the consequences. Again, the police arrived the following morning to take me back to prison but this time when they came, I told them I was my sister Sylvia and she was Kim, so at first they started to take her away. Once they realised their mistake, they came for me and in doing so, I grabbed a knife from the kitchen. What I was going to do with it, I had no idea. They quickly disarmed me and this time I wasn't so lucky and like the other girls before, I was also sent to Bullwood Hall closed prison. This was not a nice prison. You had to slop out in the mornings with your bucket of urine and faeces, rank!

I got a huge culture shock - just sixteen and pretty naïve. I didn't realise that this prison was mixed, female and males. I had to mention this to the nurse. "Eh I didn't know we 'ad mixed prisons in England?" I said. She looked at me with a straight face, but I could tell she was trying not to laugh.

"Sweetie, bless yer heart, they're not men, they're lesbians," she said. Well, now I was not only horrified but shit scared too. Oh why, oh why had Mum made me watch the film "Scrubbers"? I was just a wee young thing and these girls were massive.

Anyway, I spent a week in the hospital wing. They checked me over pretty thoroughly, and then they moved me to house four for a few days until they allocated me to a permanent wing for which they thought you would be most suited. Fuck, my luck had definitely run out because I managed to get allocated to house three, the worse wing there. Just before I moved there the kind nurse took me to one side.

"Now dear," she said. "Don't be scared because they will smell your fear. There are some nasty pieces of work in here and they prey on those that are scared. Watch yer back or someone can make your life hell."

Just what I needed to hear, but her advice made perfect sense. I understood. I vowed there and then that no one was going to intimidate me, no matter how small I was, no fucking way mate!

So this new girl on the block entered into house three with her held high. A confident stroll, smiling and acting confident. The plus side was that I had my own cell - it smelt fresh. It was very clean with its own potty and a lid. I took one look at the potty, no way was I using that. I hadn't sat on one since I was two years old and I damn sure wasn't going to start using one again. I vowed to hold it in and use the proper toilets in the mornings. Not once did I use it, even dogs don't shit where they sleep and neither would I. I tried to listen to Dad's words and keep my head down, but circumstances arose where I found myself involved in three separate brawls.

The first was when I had just been paid. I bought all my toiletries but someone entered my cell and stole them. Another inmate informed me who had stolen them so I went into her cell, smashed her in the face a few times then took back my belongings. What a fucking liberty! We were both sent to the block for fighting and I shouted through the window to her.

"Just say we were play fighting and I got carried away and I won't say nuffin' bout you knickin' me stuff," I said.

So that was our story, and we both received seven days behind the door as punishment - in other words lockdown. It didn't bother me at all. I was quite happy in my cell, cleaning it with a bar of Imperial Leather soap and using talcum powder as air freshener, it smelt lovely. I even won Cleanest Cell on the Block and everyone used to like to visit me because it smelt so fresh.

My second fight was, again, over something very trivial and, again, we each received seven days lockdown. But my last fight was totally uncalled for and bang out of order. I was asleep on my bed with the door unlocked when in walked a black girl. She just began smashing me in the face as I slept. I awoke to her ripping my hair out and punching me in the face. Worse still, I had no knowledge of why. It was totally unprovoked. I managed to try and defend myself the best I could, but she'd already smashed me about. I just got to grab a few chunks out of her hair but eventually, someone overheard the disturbance and separated us. This time, our punishment was a loss of pay and – yep - another seven days behind the door.

These brawls took place during, what I called, my Settling In Days. After that, I rarely had problems with anyone. I became quite popular amongst the other girls - always joking and laughing about. My job was Head of the Launderette, Bea Smith - ha ha. I got on particularly well with one of the prison officers, Helen from Milton Keynes. She used to bring me inside an empty Maxwell coffee jar full up with cigarette butts. I would empty the tobacco out into a tin with orange peel to moisten it. Then, I'd resell it to the new girls in quarter or half ounce batches. Yes, Kimmy was back in business running a small tobacco racket.

I was then transferred to another cell and had a few lesbians on my case. In fact, quite a few had the hots for me. I was a regular little pin up. A lot of the girls there had female relationships throughout their stay at Her Majesty's Services, but once released they would return to their boyfriends. I mainly hung around with the black girls. They were more fun, didn't take themselves too seriously unlike some of the others. I even ended up having a very quick fling with a beautiful black, Rastafarian girl. I tried it the once, I can't say it wasn't nice because it was - but I definitely preferred boys. I later found out that it was because of this girl that I had got battered by the black girl while I was sleeping. It was her girlfriend. We became good friends afterwards.

One afternoon, while working in the launderette, I declared I wanted my nose pierced. Well fuck me, everyone wanted to pierce me! I chose a friend to do the deed and I actually passed out when she was piercing me. I awoke to find a curtain ring through my nose - oh how we laughed. I looked like a farm yard bull. When my parents came to visit, Dad nearly died at the sight of the curtain ring. Eventually, I removed it but I still have that small scar where it was.

Traditionally, on visiting days, friends would shout things out of the window to any guest. My parents got to hear "Kim Farry is bent,"often enough - I laughed. I had tried it but I knew I wasn't. It was while behind bars, I also had my home made tattoo removed. I no longer liked Terry at this point because he turned into a police informant. A grass on all the local criminals. Back in those days, there was no laser surgery. They had to cut it out. Believe me, it was pure torture and the scar left behind was twice the size of the tattoo.

I am going to state the obvious here now - there was a lot of petty jealousy and shit that went on in prison. It also put my little life into perspective. So many of the girls came from terrible backgrounds. They had suffered sexual abuse, mental and physical cruelty, more often than not from their own family members. A lot of them had deliberately committed crimes and gone to prison in order to get away from their pain in the real world. I realised that at least I came from a loving family. Some of the girls never received one visitor.

I made the best of a bad situation, something I tend to do when the chips are down. There really is no point in becoming depressed and to cry in a prison. That is to admit you have a weakness. You learn to hide your inner emotions and look for the funny side of life. Laughter really is the best medicine. I was openly bothered by some things though. Some of my so-called 'close friends' didn't even bother writing to me, but others who I wouldn't consider close to me, did. Life is full of surprises and you find out who the true people are around you when the chips are down, when you have nothing to offer.

While contemplating how I was feeling behind bars, I let my guard up when some nasty, jealous bitch grassed me up about my tobacco racket, so that came to an abrupt end and I was sent down to the block yet again. Some girls would throw shit parcels out of their windows, that made my stomach churn - how revolting. We weren't allowed matches in there but would smuggle them in and split them into four to make them last longer. To smuggle them in, we used fresh cloth unpicked from new clothes in the launderette (the cloth had to be brand new unwashed or it wouldn't work). We formed cotton wool balls and tied them to a shoelace then tied that to the windows and ignited it to make night lights swinging them from window-to-window. Sometimes, we would use a tampon for cotton wool.

Remember, it was all about survival and, in many ways, to scam the system. For example, if your parents sent you the maximum of twenty pounds to spend and your cell mate had nobody sending her any money, you just arranged for whoever was sending the cash to you to send some more to your cell mate. You could have double obviously, giving her a cut of the cash. Believe me, there were many girls with nothing.

I was lucky in that I always had somebody on the outside to help me. I never had to go without.

I met some really nice girls there too. They were good friends, but my Dad's advice was never to bring the prison life home with you. He wanted me to leave it all behind and that's exactly what I did. Once home from prison, three of my fellow inmates arrived at my door looking for me. I was not home but my Dad was.

"Sorry to bovva you, is Kim home?" said one of the girls.

"Nah she ain't. She's gone to Canada to live wiv o me relatives, she ain't comin' back never, sorry girls," and he closed the door.

Well, that was the version he told me afterwards. Knowing him, he probably used harsher words and ended the conversation with, "Now fuck off an don't cum back!"

Dad could be rude but very funny too. All my mates loved him. He would repeat his same joke to my black friends, "Been sunny round your way, 'as it?" There was none of the political correctness you see today. We had a laugh though.

To date, I think I have actually been arrested about thirty times and had several 'Taken into Consideration' offences. The first time I was released and finally arrived home from the Borstal sentence, I decided to clean up my act and smarten up my shoplifting game. I had that desire to improve my stealing techniques. Going to prison did not deter me at all. I tried to go straight and work like a "normal person" but I was surrounded by a lot of jealous people. Somebody would always inform my new employers of my past and I would be sacked on the spot because they couldn't trust me. So I reverted back to my life of crime.

In my forty six years of crime, I have been imprisoned five times and each time I was released I just went back to my shoplifting. It was all I knew, my way of survival. This is going to sound weird but I loved being inside a courtroom. Maybe because I spent so many hours there whilst I was a juvenile, but over the years I adored them. It's the sense of power they held and I admired power, probably because I have always been a strong and powerful person.

Sadly, I have been surrounded by many jealous people. I really do not feel any hatred towards them. I just cannot comprehend why they have been hateful towards me. Sometimes, I am glad that I spent my life half deaf so I did not have to listen to their poisonous lies and betrayals. Really and truly, I guess they envied me so they would invent lies and slanderous comments to mask their own miserable lives. Hey, it's not my problem. I know the truth and I know who I am. What I have been through has made me a stronger person and for that I hold my head high with pride. No one has the right to judge another.

Chapter 3 - First love

At thirteen, I met my first real love, Gary. Although at first we were just mates, until a few years later when we started dating. I thought I was in love at the time. He didn't work and was from a similar background to me. He came from a huge family, even had more siblings than me. He was one of twelve children. The council had to knock two houses into one to accommodate his sister because she too had many children, and they had little money.

I lost my virginity to Gary but secretly I was besotted with his best friend Paul. Paul and I had a fling, and my heart was always with him. Sadly, he overdosed very young, so then I guess I was driven back to Gary. At nineteen, I gave birth to my eldest child Damon.

I didn't realise at the time that I was not the only woman in Gary's life. He spent his days drinking, gambling and womanising whilst I was going out stealing daily to pay for all our nice food, the bills and clothed us all. Shortly after I gave birth to Jade and then Ricky, here I was, a mother to three children whilst I was barely an adult myself and I was establishing my business, as I called it. He just took everything in his stride and expected his meals on the table. He behaved like a total wanker and never helped in looking after his own three children.

My first flat with Gary was a two bedroom maisonette in Shelford on the Cambridge Estate. The kitchen was downstairs with enough space for a table and chairs. Upstairs, to the right of the small landing, was the front room with a tiny balcony - big enough to hang out your washing and used as a lookout when someone rang the doorbell below. To the left, there was a small toilet, separate bathroom and two bedrooms.

My flat was spotless, immaculate; I cleaned it from top-to-toe every morning before I went shoplifting. I also furnished it with nice things. We never had a dull moment living there as we had people round everyday – so it seemed – especially with my family visiting and Gary's family there. When I cooked dinner, I shouted out of the window and half the estate would arrive to eat. It was an in-joke that Gary's brother and girlfriend arrived every evening without fail at dinner time. On Saturday mornings, I would be in the supermarket stealing various joints of meat for all the people I needed to feed for Sunday. Back in those days, we all seemed to muck in together. There was a real community feel, with both our families, friends and me - and my trolley. I loved to help others, whether it was clothes for their children or putting food on their tables. I would help people in need.

Apart from constantly having visitors, we seemed to always have someone lodging with us too. Friends, that for the time being, had nowhere to stay so they'd stay in the children's bedroom. Scott and Patrick spent a lot of time with me then and both stayed over a lot. Scott had a beautiful girlfriend called Jean who was a hairdresser and she spent a lot of time with us. She was plotted up in my kitchen cutting and highlighting half the residents of the estate's hair. Salt and pepper coloured hair was the fashion and she didn't highlight like they do nowadays with foil. It was a rubber hat with holes in on your head and pulling the hair through with a crochet hook. It used to hurt especially when she pulled the cap off. All the boys had the highlights too and, at one stage, she had done all the boys on Gary's football team - the same style and colour. So on the pitch, they all looked the same and nobody knew who had the ball, it was funny.

Gary's brother Ronnie was funny. If anyone did anything out of order he would insist on holding a court case in the front room and pretend to be a judge. He'd cover his head with a tea towel, put on a posh voice and ask all those involved to give evidence for or against the accused. I remember I had a girl staying with me and while she was there, she stole my son's bracelet and money from his piggy bank – fuckin' liberty mate. So Ronnie called her in and the court case began. He was a bit of a cheeky bastard and he went through her dirty laundry, picked up a pair of her dirty knickers on the end of a stick and was waving them in the air as part of the evidence. She was found guilty, partly on the state of her dirty knickers and she was sentenced to an entire week shopping with me free of charge, i.e. I didn't have to pay her. So that was a result for me.

For some bizarre reason, Gary proposed to me and I accepted. I must have had a few Jack Daniels at the time and an impaired judgement but the wedding of the year was on and I had lots to do. Unsure of which white dress to choose, I stole two. We hired a hall, a live DJ and a live band called Mirror Mirror. This was the eighties when I embraced lots of big hair and shoulder pads.

Dad helped. Because our flat on the Cambridge Estate was five minutes from his new house, I had become very close to him. Mum was still in Basingstoke and I rarely saw her. He shared the house with Maggie, his new girlfriend, and her three children. Maggie welcomed me into her home with open arms and made me very welcome. She also loved to cater for parties so she insisted on preparing all the food for the wedding. The hall we hired was two minutes from her house so she could walk it all around the corner. As a finishing touch to my requirements, I hired a chauffeur driven limousine to take me to Kingston Registry Office. A friend's brother knew another friend who had it. That's how we rolled in the eighties. Someone always knew someone to get something on the cheap.

I took orders and stole everyone's wedding outfits. Those that couldn't afford to pay, I gave them there's for free. I arranged cheap alcohol from another friend that worked in a brewery - or off license, I really couldn't remember - but all expenses I paid myself.

It was probably an omen, but I tried to back out on the day of the wedding. I stood in my Dad's house, dressed in my white dress and said, "Dad, I don't wanna do it!"

"Don't be silly Kim. It's just yer nerves, you'll be fine," he said, talking me round. I went ahead with it, but deep inside, I knew I was making a grave mistake. I was Mrs Kim Pinnock. Funnily enough, when I looked at the photos of the wedding afterwards, we seemed to be the only two not smiling.

As I came out in my dress, some female guest remarked under her breath, "Fuckin' cheek, only wearing a white dress!" I didn't hear her because I would have smashed her face in and ruined the day, but my Dad overheard her and gave the woman a volley of abuse. She did have a point. I had three children by then but, what a fucking liberty!

The party when on until dawn. Maggie and my Dad ran the bar like professionals. The music was great, the food was fabulous. Everyone had a fantastic time. The only one unhappy was me, "What the fuck had I done?" I asked myself. I married a playboy and was trying to establish my business whilst raising three small children. One of my favourite record albums at the time was Carol Thompson tune 'Hopelessly in Love'. The lyrics seemed to apply to me especially the line, "No you don't know how to love me."

So, what came next after marrying the wrong man? I immersed myself into my shoplifting. It became the entire focus of my existence, but I never realised back then that it was becoming a major problem - an addiction. I genuinely treated it as a proper business although I knew it was still illegal. It was the only thing I thought I could do. I was stealing from shops and stealing to order. I had no shortage of customers. This was all while Gary was drinking, gambling and shagging (I found out later).

He also stole, with a few of his mates, but he was never really that good at it. No way was he as dedicated. He was too lazy. He preferred that I was the provider for the family. However, my addiction for stealing was getting out of control. I would get up super early, at six am, clean the house thoroughly then off to 'work' when the shops opened at nine. I spent seven days a week stealing and it began to overtake my mind. All I could think about was new ways to enter and leave shops super quickly. My mind was forever ticking over with new ideas to become better at my chosen profession. I will elaborate on my schemes later in the book.

By the end of my career, forty six years later, I had mastered shoplifting to perfection. That may sound pretty pathetic and I make no excuses. I know what I did was wrong but at that time of my life, it was the only thing I seemed good at and I became obsessed in my head – alright, maybe by greed too.

I wanted to create my shopping empire, stolen shopping empire. I never realised that it would get in the way of true happiness and my ability to raise my children, but it did, and I cannot turn back time. I had been a surrogate mother to my brothers and sisters nearly my entire life and here I was then, having three children of my own - three beautiful children. My shoplifting was obstructing my ability to be a good mother to them. I constantly hired babysitters and spent nearly all day in the shops so I could steal. I am by no means justifying my actions as a parent, but a few years later, I made the conscious decision to walk away from my children and let them have a stable life. I was an animal in the shops. I was greedy and took way too much. Being small, and sometimes coming across something I couldn't reach, I would ask a taller person to get it down for me. Then, it was mine. I had determination, and once my mind was set that I wanted this 'thing', I had to have it and would not stop until I did.

The police were regular visitors and would raid the flat many times. I recall on one occasion, Mum had been babysitting. We were in the kitchen making tea when we saw them approaching the flat. I had a mountain of stolen clothes scattered around the kitchen.

"Quick Mum, stuff the gear in the tumble dryer and washing machine while I stall 'em at the door."

Poor Mum was a nervous wreck. She was not cut out for crime, but she managed to stuff them all away and they didn't find them.

They did, however, confiscate items from my kitchen cupboards - bloody cheek!

"Are you Kim?" asked a fresh faced young policeman.

"Nahh mate, she ain't 'ere" I replied.

He obviously didn't know who I was. I was not going anywhere without my solicitor with me.

"In that case, you´ll have to come with us," he said to my Mum. "Just until we locate the whereabouts of Kim." He then escorted my Mum to Kingston police station.

I watched as they took Mum away. I know, as I write this, I was pretty out of order to let her go to the police station. After all, she hadn't even done anything, except babysit. They kept her there for four hours - fucking liberty! They couldn't prove that the luxury kitchen items they had removed were stolen so a friend with my solicitor went to collect them. My so-called friend tried to tell me that the police were keeping the items but I knew different. The cheeky cow had taken them back to her house to keep. I saw through her lies and promptly strolled round to her house and took them all back. Another liberty taker, I guess because we were all thieves, some people had no limits. There didn't seem too much honour amongst thieves.

The downside of my lifestyle was that I never had time for any real friends or quality of life. By that, I am not referring to material things. I mean true friends. I just had people that seemed to come into my life then leave just as quickly. Nobody really remained because my addiction made me just eat, sleep and breathe shopping. Nothing else mattered, I mean nothing. Over the years I have fallen in and out of love with boyfriends, friends and even family members. To this day, I have only one true loyal friend and that is my good friend Michelle Beer and her children. She, I can honestly say, has always been there for me, through thick and thin, for many years.

I truly believed that because I wasn't harming anyone, stealing from the shops was acceptable. I declared war on Kingston town shopping centre. I became the queen of shopping, but in my case it was shoplifting and soon got the reputation of Kimmy's catalogue. People would order goods from me and I would deliver them within twenty four hours, a bit like Amazon Prime. I had orders that varied enormously - from household goods, designer clothes, pushchairs, prams and even furniture. I was totally self-taught. I may have watched Fagin in action once or twice. I was mastering my 'career' which I was brilliant at. I enjoyed it too. I loved the buzz of getting away with my crimes.

I thought I had everything that I wanted. I was even holding Kimmy's catalogue Tupperware parties only instead of Tupperware, it was stolen clothes - and they were very popular. I would have been in my mid-twenties by then and would spend all week collecting Kimmy's new range. I even supplied clothes rails, and other stuff were in baskets like the real shops. Whoever hosted the party received payment, usually around sixty pounds. I would generally earn around one thousand pounds. Dad and Maggie hosted a few with their bedroom stuffed with stolen clothes. People even went into the bathroom to try things on. I sometimes gave the hosts commission which gave them more incentive to sell the merchandise.

The very best sales assistant was Sylvia because she definitely had the gift of the gab. Oh yes, Sylvia could chat you into buying a pair of pyjamas when all you wanted was a new dress! I never had any shortage of would-be employees because I knew so many unemployed people that could all benefit with a bit of extra cash in their pockets. Plus, they got new clothes and food thrown in the deal and could earn between sixty to eighty pounds an hour.

In order to improve my shoplifting, I needed wheels. I wanted to learn to drive. So, I bought an old car to teach myself to drive. Oh my God, on the first day I decided to take my son, Damon, to nursery school in Kingston. Well, how I didn't get stopped by the police, to this day I will never know. I kangarooed all the way there, then kangarooed all the way back. The car jumped there and back! By the time I got home, it was time to return to collect Damon – I was that slow.

On another day, Sylvia came for a ride but by the time we reached our destination I had forgotten how to stop the car and we nearly hit the wall. We both screamed simultaneously, just as I managed to stop in time. I sure was crazy in my younger days.

Eventually, I traded that car for an automatic Ford Escort. It was far easier to drive. I managed to find a place in New Malden that taxed and insured it fully, despite the fact that I didn't even hold a driving license. How was that even possible? I then drove from Kingston to Basingstoke to visit Mum. She couldn't believe that I had arrived alive! I never got stopped by the police so I was under the illusion that I must be a good driver. I thought I was the dogs bollocks. I was finally moving up in the world, the world was my oyster. Before, I had to pay people to drive me about shopping. Now I was, as my Dad used to say, "speculate to accumulate", investing in my future shopping ventures.

So there I was - in my twenties, and married to a man that seemed to be a pretty useless husband and provider. Then, I was stealing on a daily basis, partly to get my buzz and also to compensate for the marriage I felt was falling apart. I would visit the shops in advance, locating the cameras, the exits and the merchandise I needed to access, so that when I entered, I wouldn't be flapping about. Just go in and out quickly with little time to be noticed. I wore disguises - wigs and makeup so I blended in with the clientele, or sometimes even the staff. I did work unofficially in one shop for a year wearing the staff's uniform, but I was caught helping someone out. I will explain that later.

Being 'at work', I was quite a phenomenon. Any of my past accomplices would agree I was fast and efficient. No doubt some may come forward with their own stories. There are way too many to remember. I arranged my entire life around retail opening hours and expected those that worked with me to do the same. I fell out with a few because "they were busy". What did they mean "busy"? I had no time for anything except shopping. I had no interest in family days out. As far as I was concerned, whilst the shops were open, I was earning my living. A day out meant losing money. I loved what I did and if I wasn't working, there was cooking and cleaning to take care of.

My addiction was taking me beyond the concept of reality. I believed I could get what I wanted, when I wanted. In believing this, it totally twisted my values in life. They were all topsy-turvy, yet I couldn't see it - just fucked up!

As I mentioned earlier, about the unofficial working in two department stores, I shall elaborate. I dressed as a member of staff, copied their uniforms and was able to help myself to thousands of pounds worth of goods. Nobody questioned my identity. I was bold, brazen, blended in and super confident. The more brazen I was, the more I seemed to get away with things.

Returning to my life with Gary, he was my first serious love and at the beginning we used to laugh and laugh, and have fun. We were just kids when we met, playing at being grown up. After the children were born, things seemed to change for the worse. We were constantly arguing and usually in front of the three very small children in the small flat. I avoided sex by using my period as an excuse and used to wear sanitary towels to make it seem real. I tried to compensate for the failure of my marriage by filling the flat with nice things and I thought that would improve things, but it didn't. I was no longer in love with Gary. The rumours started about his other flings, which didn't help. Sometimes, these flings were with my so-called friends. Oh how I want to name and shame them, but it's many moons ago. They did me a favour.

Then I met Gary's friend Jim Stokes. We hit it off immediately. He actually paid attention to me whenever I spoke, something Gary didn't do. In time, and I'm not super proud of this, but Jim and I became secret lovers. I would pretend to go shoplifting and instead meet with Jim during the day. I was secretly saving money to leave Gary and the children. I even bought a new stereo system and television for the flat just before I left. Fuck knows why - I knew I was leaving. I hated deceiving Gary and had tried to leave him before when I fled to Mum's in Basingstoke, but he just followed me there and brought me home. He was a proper stalker. I could not shake him off. He must have sensed something because one morning, after a night out with friends, he accused me of flirting with Jim. I denied it, of course. But then, bang, he punched me straight in the mouth and cut my lip. I was only wearing my dressing gown and slippers, nothing underneath and it was winter time, but I just walked straight out of the flat round to Dad's on the other side of the estate. Eventually Gary came and got me and brought me back home.

That wasn't the first time he had hit me. On another occasion, I was having a girly sisters afternoon with Sylvia and Tracy. Tracy gave me a makeover because I rarely wore makeup and when Gary returned, he was furious and drop kicked me in the face.

Chapter 4 - Jim Stokes

Jim and I eloped to Spain, Menorca to be precise. We flew with a friend Phil Bullen and we had an amazing time. For the first time in years, I forgot about shopping, cooking, cleaning. I felt free and happy. Gary was apparently distraught and looking for me everywhere. He had to look after the children and wasn't coping very well, so Maggie and Dad agreed to have little Ricky because he was only nine months old. Dad took to Ricky instantly and began calling him "My little man". Maggie was an amazing and warm lady and never once judged me for leaving the children.

Of course, all good things come to an end and it was time for us to return to England. Then, shit really did hit the fan - it was vile. While Gary had been searching for me, various other family members had been looking after Damon and Jade. His sister had Damon and my brother Patrick and his girlfriend Anna looked after Jade. Upon our return, it was now that the entire Pinnock clan turned into my enemies. This carried on for months. They bullied Jim and I, never minded that I was treated like dirt throughout my marriage to their brother.

Our cars were smashed up, they slashed the tyres, that wasn't a problem. I had money so that was easily repairable. But the situation felt so bad, I made a conscious decision to leave my children. My lifestyle, the way I shopped and lived was not a very secure environment to raise children so I chose to walk away.

The dust had settled a little and Gary moved on with a new girlfriend and took back Damon and Jade. She was obviously taking care of them. Ricky remained with Dad, Maggie and her three children and was very settled in his new life. Then, Gary suddenly declared he could no longer cope with Damon and Jade and I believe the girlfriend at the time did not treat them properly. Maggie persuaded Dad that they should provide a loving and caring home for the three children. She did not want to see them disappear into the welfare system or get split up. This was not decided overnight. It took a lot of indepth conversations with Dad and Maggie. I knew, and they knew, that I couldn't provide them with a stable lifestyle, a lifestyle that children needed.

I was not willing to give up stealing even for my own children. My own selfishness needed to shoplift. It had caused a wedge and there was my new boyfriend to consider. It was a mess. We all concluded that they would benefit from being raised by their Grandad, my Dad and Maggie. Hell, that was one of the hardest decisions I have ever had to make in my life. But I knew it was in the children's interest because I was clearly not in the right place to raise three children.

So I walked away. It was heart wrenching but I still maintain it was the best thing I could do for them. They turned out to be great children.

Gary was clearly deranged that I had left and continued to hassle me. Many months later, when I was five months pregnant with my son Jimmy, I was in the Cinderella's Nightclub and Gary was there too. He tried to attack me inside the club so the bouncers got me out the back door. Jim was livid and so took revenge. He waited for him after football practice outside a pub then when Gary emerged, he battered him.

Later, Gary's family retaliated by breaking into my new flat in New Malden and smashed things. Nobody was home. They also stole things but missed the wads of cash I hid in the drawers. We seemed to be at war with the family for years they just would not let it go. But, every cloud has silver lining. Gary and I did manage to produce three beautiful children, that I do not regret.

I agreed for Dad and Maggie to officially obtain a custody order for the three children. Gary agreed too. So we all had to attend a court hearing at The Strand, granting them the order. Dad also asked me to stay away from the children for a while so that they could get accustomed to their new lives and settle in without emotional heartbreak interfering. They didn't want them confused about why they were not with Mummy so coming and going into their lives was not an option. I agreed and phoned my Dad regularly and popped round to visit when I knew the kids were either at school or late when they were sleeping.

I would never visit them empty handed. I always came with bin liners of toys or new clothes, whatever the children needed. I also helped with money and food, I even paid for a new carpet. I couldn't get too close to them at this early stage of their lives so I helped out when I could. Then, I did what I'd always do when hurt - I went on major shoplifting sprees and got a shit load of buzz going on, and threw myself into 'my business'.

Gary never really helped out financially nor mentally. He eventually settled with a girl and they moved to Orpington together. Years later, they separated and he was entitled to half the sale of their house. He promised Damon, Ricky and Jade that he would be giving them some money but they never saw one penny. He still was a waste of space all those years later. My

Dad was their 'Dad' and I knew it broke each of their hearts when he died. Sadly, Maggie died eight years later.

I was, and am, happy for the way those three children turned out. They had a far better upbringing away from me. I am certain many of you and Jeremy Kyle would say, "Why have children in the first place?" My answer is that I never intended for things to turn out the way they did. Things just happened and I (as I am sure a lot of young people do) never thought things through back then. By placing them in Dad's care was the best solution – so, fuck you all on that one.

I am not made of stone. I have feelings and sobbed about how I abandoned them. Now they are older, I hold a close bond with all three children. Our past makes us who we are today, especially our mistakes, and I am quite happy with that. Dad and Maggie did a far better job than I could have done. I made the best decision for them.

Jim Stokes was pretty quiet and reserved. He had a nervous twitch with his eyes that, apparently, he only developed when he met me. After we separated years later, the twitch disappeared. He was a pipe fitter by trade but used to work in the Kingston fish market. Hence, he was alright about a fishy fanny – not -

only joking. The crude side of my sense of humour is coming out now! He was a fit guy and took care of his health but yet again I was the bread winner of the house. Although he worked, he could be a bit of a tight arse with his money. He would buy me nice, sexy underwear, something that he would benefit from. But he'd never say, "Here you go. Go and treat yourself," and give me wad of cash.

I adored and worshipped Jim, and loved him with all my heart. At least, I thought I did at the time. He used to tease me because he liked busty girls and since giving birth to the three children, mine were small, he called me fried eggs so I used to retaliate by cutting out the Page 3 models' pictures from The Sun newspaper. He couldn't believe that I would do such a thing but he gave me a complete complex about my boobs. Before my first breast enhancement, I always stuffed my bras with cotton wool before getting ready for a night out. Once I had my new boobs, I was so proud of them that I could not stop exposing myself and showing them off at every opportunity I had. I became a regular flasher. I would be in a nightclub on the stage, dancing (I was the queen of Options nightclub at one stage) and after a few drinks, then bang out came my boobs on display.

As you can see, I liked shocking people. One night, I stuck my boobs on the window of an Indian Restaurant and the whole restaurant began laughing. The owners invited me inside for a free drink. Jim and I were together for seven years and shared a flat in Martin House, New Malden. Again, I took to refurbishing the flat with luxury items. I ripped out the bathroom and had a carpenter install tongue and groove cladding and gold fittings taps. It looked like a Swedish sauna but it was the fashion at the time, honest!

Once we moved into this flat, I branched out into stealing homeware and furniture. I began to steal pine chests of drawers, huge mirrors, rugs, pictures, lamps and fixtures and fittings from B&Q. Kitchenware basically. If I could lift it, I would take it. In some cases, where I couldn't lift it but desperately wanted it, I would pay a strapping young man to lift the item for me. I even managed to steal our television. I have always taken pride in my home, and always will, but I never bragged to people about my home. Well, until now.

Jim and I had a very healthy sex life and I was never shy to initiate a bit of fun. I did, and still do, love sex. A few times, we chose to go risqué and liked to have sex spontaneously outdoors. Richmond Park was one of my favourite venues. We had sex with Jim full monty in the park being watched by the randy deers and wildlife. Well, I'd like to think they were the only ones watching. Who knows - it was so intense, there could have been a few passers-by. Another time, we actually got caught having sex in the car at Richmond Park car park but I was never red faced. I thought it was funny. It was always my idea. I am pretty confident when it comes to making my partners happy.

I was, as per usual, serious about my shoplifting and finally got caught. This time, I was sentenced to six months in prison. During my time there, I became friends with a beautiful lady called Maria. When I say beautiful, she was a stunning brunette with a figure to die for. She should have been a model, and we soon became 'as thick as thieves'!

Once released, every Thursday evening during the late night shopping, Maria and I would each load up a trolley with food in Marks & Spencer. Then we'd take the trolleys, once laden with stolen food into the lifts, and directly into the car park where we frantically tipped all the shopping into the car and sped away at high speed with enough food to last the week. We were so quick, we perfected this scam and speed was the essence.

The scam carried on for about a year. As all good things come to an end, this one did too. We somehow had changed from our regular Thursday shopping trip to a Friday, so that was a bad omen for a start. Anyway, I noticed that we had been seen and were being followed by the store detectives, or as I call them, 'the undies'. I immediately abandoned my trolley full of groceries and told her to do the same. She wouldn't listen to me and got in the lift heading towards the parked car. As soon as we came out of the lift, the undie pounced on us. She was female and I jumped on her back like a monkey. Fuck knows why. It was just my reaction but she had already radioed for backup and others arrived. We were both arrested.

I was the first to appear in court and received a five month sentence. Maria appeared before the judge two weeks later and she was sentenced based on my criminal record. They really were not allowed to do that but they did anyway, and she received a five month sentence too. We met up in Holloway Prison and to begin with, we shared a cell. We were having so much fun, laughing all the time. That annoyed the guards and we were soon separated.

I knew Maria had dabbled in drugs when I first met her, but never really grasped the concept of how much she took until one day, soon after we were released, I walked in on her chasing the dragon. I was horrified.

"What the fuck are you doin', Maria. Get a fucking grip."

She just stared at me with a glaze in her eyes and her pupils were pinned out. I tried in vain to help her but to no avail. She became a full on junkie. The heroin took its toll and destroyed my friend and our friendship. She was holding six hundred pounds of mine and apparently it got "stolen". Well, I gave her a deadline to return my money and she did. But, trust disappears once the drug takes over people's brains. It becomes about survival and a mountain of lies. Her looks rapidly disappeared and I could no longer be associated with her.

A few years later, two of Maria's daughters became addicts and they were beauties too. As I write this, she is still alive and I sometimes bump into her. Sadly, she has never managed to get clean. Just one moment of weakness can ruin your life. She said to me years ago, "Kim where did I go wrong?"

I walked away with tears in my eyes.

Unfortunately, she was not my only friend I lost in the abyss of the drug world. I had another accomplice working with me and she didn't know what to do with all the money she had. She spent her entire life in poverty and she began wasting it on drugs and became addicted to crack. Like Maria, we parted our ways. It was such a shame. She was so young and had her entire life ahead of her and I watched her deteriorate before my eyes.

I found out I was pregnant whilst in Holloway Prison. They gave me an internal to establish how many weeks I was but it induced me into labour and I lost the child. These days, I suppose I could probably file a law suit against the prison doctor. I was in so much pain and it didn't help that my cell mate was super religious and holding a prayer vigil at the bottom of my bed. I thought "Fuck me, I'm dying." In the end, they took me to hospital.

Shortly after my release from prison, I fell pregnant again. Jim was not convinced we were ready to be parents but I insisted on going through with the pregnancy. I gave birth to a beautiful baby boy, Jimmy. After the birth of our son, things seemed to change dramatically between us. It was as though we just started to drift apart. Jim had lost interest in me and I was rapidly losing interest in him. I began partying hard with friends, drinking and taking recreational drugs. I was, again, going into a bad place mentally and we eventually separated. I decided that again I was not fit to be a mother. Maybe I rushed into it too soon. I thought a baby would bring us closer together but it did exactly the reverse and drove us apart.

So like before, I chose to walk away and baby Jimmy was raised by Jim's parents, his grandparents, Val and Stan. I drove there that day, handed them my son and said, "Please look after him and don't let anyone else take him away." And they did and, like Dad and Maggie with my first three, were fantastic. He is great now and is a grown man. A qualified electrician. He has a great head for mathematics like my Dad. He definitely doesn't get his maths skills from his own father.

Unlike the other three children, I had no contact with Jimmy at all until he became fifteen when he became curious about his real mother. I kept my ears to the ground because I knew a few of Jimmy's neighbours so received regular reports of how he was growing up over the years. He is a credit to Val and Stan - they love him with all their hearts.

There had been a few dramas regarding Jimmy over the years, mainly due to the fact that his Dad couldn't bear being in the same room as me. He seems to despise me with a passion. Even after twenty years, he never brought himself to act civil around me. Perhaps he still had feelings for me? Who knows. But he could have, at least, made the effort for young Jimmy's sake and move on with his life. I have! Move on, mate! I knew that when the time was right, then my son would come and find me and he did. Thankfully, we mended our bridges and made up for lost time.

Chapter 5 - Breakdown

Just after I split up from Jim, I was regularly at Options nightclub and loved to dance the night away. I was about twenty six years old or twenty seven. One Thursday night, I got together with a few friends and we were having a great night as usual. I was up on stage dancing and felt fantastic and had a brilliant night. When I returned home, I began to feel out of sorts, a little strange. Then I began to hallucinate. I could see flowers coming out of the wall and my quilt cover. I screamed. The guy I was with woke up.

"What the fuck's wrong, Kim. Why are you screaming?" he asked.

"Why am I screaming? There's fuckin' flowers coming out the wall an' me quilt!"

"Jesus Christ! Someone's spiked yer drink, or you drunk the wrong one."

I could hear what he was saying but my brain couldn't comprehend his words. I did not like this weird feeling and panic set inside me. I jumped out of the bed and headed towards the door.

"Where the fuck are ya goin', Kim?" he said.

"I dunno, but I've gotta get out of 'ere."

I ran out of the front door heading towards the busy road. I was actually walking in the middle of Kingston Road in the early hours of the morning in my nightwear like an escaped mental patient, eyes wide open. Luckily at that hour, there were hardly any cars on the road. By chance, friends of mine Carol and Graham were passing and stopped.

"What the fuck are ya doin', Kim?"

I couldn't answer. I couldn't speak properly, so they took me home and called my brother Patrick. He arrived with Anna, his wife, and they took me to the emergency unit at Kingston Hospital. As we approached the entrance, there were two workmen carrying scaffolding. I rushed forward to attack them. Patrick grabbed me, "Kim, what the fuck are ya doin'?"

"They're gonna get me with the scaffolding poles and there's a fuckin' alien inside me. Get it out, get it out!" I screamed.

"Just calm down," Patrick said holding me tight so I couldn't run off. I seriously thought everyone was trying to kill me and plotting against me. The aliens started appearing everywhere.

The hospital wanted to section me but Patrick said no and decided to take me to Dad's house. Maybe he could reason with me, or talk some sense into me. As Patrick put me in the back seat and started to drive to Dad's house, I lunged forward, muttering some incoherent words and grabbed the steering wheel, nearly sending us off the road into oncoming traffic.

"Kim, fuck off. Sit the fuck down. Yer gonna kill us."

When we arrived at Dad's house and he saw the state of me, he couldn't cope with it. He didn't want the children to see me in that state so he told Patrick to take me somewhere else until she feels better. So Patrick drove me to Sylvia's house and she managed to sort me out, despite the fact I was still gibbering absolute nonsense. I even had an out-of-body experience, a bit like Scrooge in A Christmas Carol. I was at my own funeral and could see all the people grieving for me - not a great turn out, I have to say - no it was packed, ha. I managed to calm down, waiving off the effects of the drugs after drinking a shitload of orange juice.

The whole experience, I found a few weeks later, was because I had picked up the wrong drink and the one that I drank contained a strip of acid meant for someone else. I've never left my drink unattended ever since. Let that be a warning to all you youngsters out there, especially with these rape drugs available. After that, I hibernated for six months having lost the urge to go partying. I even cut all my hair short.

Chapter 6 - Jerry Proctor

Well, what can I say about Jerry? He was an exceptional man who I first met when I walked into his solicitors practice in Pearson's, New Malden High Street. He was average height with sharp features but had a warm glow about him. I cannot explain it, but as a solicitor, he was really trustworthy. He was like no other solicitor I had ever met before. I must have been in my twenties and living with Jim at the time. At that moment, I took an instant like to this new man and he became my solicitor for sixteen years.

Our relationship was a substance of real friendship and I really did come to care about Jerry. I recommended him to every small time crook I knew and he was soon inundated with so many cases, he left the New Malden Office and opened his own firm with his own secretary in Kingston's Market Place. I could always tell him the truth about my cases and he always provided me with the very top barristers to fight my corner. He genuinely cared about all his clients and not just some money making lawyer.

We had a wonderful, and completely platonic, relationship - contrary to many people's gossip and tongue wagging. We were never involved in a sexual way. If anything, he took me under his wing as a father figure. He managed my criminal affairs for many years before we became really good friends. It was at a stage in my life when I had no boyfriend and although I had gone to prison and left my sister Tammy in charge of my house and teenage children Danny and Jade, I had lost everything.

I was basically on my arse. All I had built over the years I had lost. Even down to my underwear and my house was trashed. Jerry picked me back up from my despair. He knew beforehand that my home had been ruined. Even as I came out of the prison gates, he was waiting to take me home. It was laughable then as I had no home to go back to. How he knew, I had no idea. He also knew he had to give me the tragic news, I had lost everything. The bricks and mortar were the only things left.

I then was invited to appear on the Kilroy Show. The topic of the day was shoplifting. Kilroy asked me what it would take to retire from stealing and I replied jokingly, "A sugar daddy". The show was a bit hairy because I was sitting next to a female police officer and was convinced that the minute the show finished, she would have me in handcuffs. I also had to deal with the audience shouting "I blame her parents!" How dare they blame my parents. I did what I did myself - nothing to do with them at all.

I mimicked the critics, saying things like "Maybe you should take up stealing, looking at the state of your clothes." It was my defence mechanism. After the show was aired, Jerry watched it and called me. He was worried about me. He said I no longer needed to steal and that he could help me out financially. He was basically offering to be my sugar daddy, but without the sex! I was like "hell yes", and our friendship moved to another level. He had a beautiful wife and family and they lived in a big house in Cobham. Apparently, his mother had wanted him to be a doctor and never quite accepted his chosen profession of mixing with criminals. He was also a member of the masons - nudge, nudge, wink, wink.

He also tipped me off to warn a local family, friends I had grown up with, that the police had an undercover operation and were watching their house. After I warned them, the cheeky bastards didn't even say thank you. That's life!

He took me shopping and spent nine hundred pounds on me. He bought birthday presents for my children, paid my phone bills on standing order and purchased food for the house - anything to stop me shoplifting. For a while, it worked. But my addiction got the better of me and I soon reverted to stealing. I would help him out by explaining the criminals' point of view in some of his cases. He even took me to The Old Bailey to help on a case and then paid me generously for my time. He used me to study the mind of a criminal and the way I thought.

Jerry became a regular visitor at my house, popping in for coffee and I would give him my thoughts on certain cases he was working on. He even came to Dad's house a couple of times. Dad pulled him to one side, "Are you sleeping with my daughter?" he asked.

"No Tom, I am not. She is a lovely girl and I am quite smitten with her, but she has made it pretty clear that our relationship is purely platonic."

Deep down, I knew Jerry wanted more. I just wasn't attracted to him in that way. I liked our friendship the way it was. I decided I wanted to become a dancer at String Fellows so Jerry paid for my boob job, then gave me five hundred pounds to spend on money for underwear for the interview. I attended their interview and men kept asking me to dance. Yet, I kept bursting out in fits of laughter so it really wasn't the job for me. I had a great night and obviously enjoyed my new banging boobs for many years.

One afternoon, I guess I should have seen it coming. Jerry came to visit me at home and offered me ten thousand pounds to have sex with him. I declined the offer. Wow that was shitloads of money, but I knew it would spoil our friendship and wasn't the right thing to do. He supported me financially for a solid three years - a lot more than any of my previous three relationships had done. After that our relationship was never quite the same and not long after I met my fourth serious boyfriend, Dave Miller, Jerry just stopped the contact and we drifted apart. The sad thing is, I heard a few years later he died quite young and unexpected. I feel like I never got the chance to say goodbye.

Chapter 7 – Shopping

Throughout this chapter, if I refer to my shopping, I clearly mean shoplifting, stealing or taking without paying. As I've said before, I treated shopping like any other person would treat their own company. I had strict standards to maintain and my employee's appearance and time keeping reflected on me as The Boss. They received on the job training, had a certain dress code and strictly (in the later years, when everyone had them) no mobile phones for personal use - only for me to call them. Loyalty, as well as the ability to keep your mouth shut if you were arrested, were the top qualities I required. I would pay their fines and looked out for them as long as they looked out for me. They also had a trial period or they were simply told their services were no longer required. Just like any legal job, I was a perfectionist.

Over the years, I had many trainees. Some chose to go it alone after training but lacked my in-built instinct and usually ended up in prison. Others became as good as me and that was an achievement because it took me years. The ability to listen was a major factor too. I put one hundred percent into my business. If my accomplices did not pull their weight, or act how

I trained them to, they got the sack - simple as that. I did not have time to mess about with people who clearly were not suited to my criminal actions. Time was money! There was never a shortage of eager people ready to earn extra cash. People were easily replaced.

The dress code was no bright colours - dark and neutral colours were acceptable. Navy blue, beige, black, grey, blue and white were alright, but nothing that made you stand out from the crowd. You needed to become invisible, and no hoodies or tracksuits. Smart attire only. I would dress differently and forever change my hairstyles, apply fresh makeup. It sometimes depended on what shops I was going into. I'd wear suits for designer shops and always well groomed. If my employees had a car, they needed to be fully legal with all taxes and MOT's up-to-date. Never, under any circumstances, should they collect a parking ticket - all oyster cards and parking paid in advance.

It only took one small detail out of place to blow everything we were doing. If I caught anyone using their phone for private messages or calls, they were immediately sacked. I needed their full attention at all times. Anyone that didn't abide by my rules and regulations would receive one warning, then they were gone and quickly replaced.

Some people just weren't cut out to steal. Others were natural thieves and stayed with me for a few years. I was very well respected by many in my hometown, even some of the police and security guards used to joke around with me. There were those who hated my guts because I used to slip through the net getting away on numerous occasions. I managed to escape from many dramas because of my instinct and I was quick and good at stealing. I rarely took chances. If I ever sensed something was wrong, or that I had been seen, I abandoned mission and left the goods, kicking them under somewhere inside the shop and exiting empty handed. I relied on my eyes, my body to block things, my brain, and the fact that I can lip read. These helped me see more than others and I would also never engage in conversations with people.

I knew Kingston like the back of my hand. I'd know every single road, alleyway, short cut and all the back streets. I was chased hundreds of times but mostly got away. It was as though I used to taunt them all to catch me.

I'd take days off from shopping. I calmed down a bit when older and stopped working seven days a week. I would still look around the shops. The minute I entered any shop in Kingston, security would begin to follow me. To me, this was hilarious because I knew I was not going to steal anything. I had let them see me. I had no intention of stealing and would sometimes strike up conversations with them. "You're the nuts, Farry," they used to say. I would reply, "Of course," then cackle with laughter.

"But you need to go elsewhere, cos everyone here knows you!"

"Yeah, who don't know who I am? But you lot are all shit at yer jobs and can´t catch me!"

Most of them would have a chat and a laugh. Not all the security guards were like that. Like I said before, I was sure to be on some of their death wishlists, particularly two – one in Bentalls and the John Cleese lookalike from John Lewis who I tried to run over. I bet they were all gutted that I have retired. All I can say is, I was always one step ahead. And yes, they really were crap at their jobs.

The Kingston police despised me and wanted to get me so badly. Any new Old Bill were immediately notified of my existence and shown my photo. Another stipulation for my staff was that nobody discussed business with others out of our working circle. There were far too many jealous people around, just waiting to see me fall and fall hard.

I used my mobile phone to coordinate my staff. First, I would enter the store using my body to block anyone's view, and then load up all the bags with stolen goods. Next, a quick phone call to my accomplices to inform them of my exact location in the store so they could meet me, collect the bags and walk the stolen goods out of the exit. They would collect the bags and leave in the matter of one minute. The faster, the better. Timing was crucial.

I knew where all cameras were located in every shop I entered and also identified the camera's blind spots. I used to take everything - coats, dresses, homeware, and jackets - whatever I wanted. Hollister was one of my favourite shops because you could return goods up to four hundred pounds with no receipt and they would give you the equivalent in vouchers. I earned thousands from that store and Gilly Hicks.

Initially, I would shop on a daily basis but as the years went on, I toned it down to just the weekends. The busier the better, more people to blend in with. Christmas was the same. During the week, I would drive people around returning the stolen merchandise in exchange for vouchers but I had to be careful because there, as I said before, is no honour among thieves and a few people tried to rip me off. They soon realised they messed with the wrong person when I confronted them. I am not generally a violent person but when push comes to shove, I can lose my shit big time. Believe me, you do not want to be around when that happens - you may want to dive for cover! Needless to say I would always get the goods returned and they never messed with me again.

I'd rage over little things. Some days, an employee would say, "Oh, I can't make it today" to which I saw red.

"What the fuck? Just get in the car," I'd say, though a bit harsher. I could not risk having stolen goods sitting about.

I dreaded the sales. I must be the only person in the world that loathes the sales. Gap was a nightmare for reducing things. Some of my clients would accept goods and return them to exchange for a different outfit or the vouchers. If they left it a while then the value of the goods would be half price and they no longer had a bargain. Many complained to me. If it was a genuine complaint and they'd say the shop had reduced the items' value within a few days then I would give them the benefit of the doubt and refund the difference. But if it was a week or so later, not my problem, fuck off! No way, they were taking the piss.

Just writing about all this is giving me a few goosebumps and the urge to go shopping, I cannot lie. I miss the buzz. It's crazy, the amount of goods I could obtain in just one day. Customers would order the impossible and I would always deliver. I never realised that I was actually a kleptomaniac and basically sick until I tried to stop and realised that I did in fact need help. I always thought I was in control of my life, shopping, housework, cooking a homemade meal every night. I have always been on top of everything and a very active person.

I killed (as in I robbed them blind) Gilly Hicks, Hollister's, John Lewis, and Bentalls. I do love a Bentalls quilt set or ten. When I was eleven years old, I was caught stealing some baby clothes for a friend and a Marc Bolan badge for me in Bentalls. So once older, and better skilled, I took out my revenge out on Bentalls. I would enter the store dressed in a black suit like their employees. I then went behind the till taking empty Bentalls bags then fill them up with designer goods and pass them to my employees to take out of the store and load into the car. I would remain inside to repeat the same and stay there until basically I had enough or the car was full up. Sometimes, we would go home unload the car then return for another session. We would take whatever I fancied or people had ordered - menswear, womenswear, children's wear, homeware and clothes for ourselves. We had wardrobes to die for and wads of money. Life was good. Obviously I made the most money and I gave each of my employees a wage. Mr Bentalls, don't you just love me!

I cannot begin to tell you every story because there are far too many. I shall try and give you an insight into my normal 'working day'. I would meet my accomplices in the town centre early, then we would begin stealing from the shops. I repeated the bag-collecting method, by replicating the strategy I'd use for Bentalls, in all the shops I stole from. It looks less suspicious if you are carrying a bag with the shops logo past security full of merchandise. As well as Bentalls, Hollister's and Gilly Hicks, my other favourite stores were Next, New Look, Boots, Republic, Topman, Topshop, Burtons, Miss Selfridge, Mothercare, H&M, JD Sports, Gap, Laura Ashley and HMV Records. I would frequently visit these shops on a daily basis. Once I had tagged and bagged it, I would get the others to return it all for the vouchers and sometimes walk away with two to three thousand pounds worth of vouchers per day. Occasionally, they would refund cash but not very often.

The rules used to be, up to three hundred pound exchange per person for the vouchers. Later, the shops began to lower the limit per person. Each of my girls earned ten pounds per exchange which they were more than happy with. All over and done with quickly, I liked to operate early in the morning. This went on for years and the word spread around so soon, everybody wanted to work for me and so my illegal empire grew.

My list of clients changed too. It was no longer the poor and needy, but I also had professional people placing orders for the vouchers - lawyers, teachers, fitness instructors, and well off mothers - really well to do people. Or, as I call them, the posh people. The vouchers were in demand. Other clients were happy for me to pick out clothes for them as I always had an eye for what would suit certain people. I would shop with their figure and style in my head. I was Gok Wan-ing people way before he was. If I was asked to get one hundred pounds worth of new wardrobe for someone's ten year old son, I would deliver. I seem to know what suits people. Maybe I needed a job in fashion. After all, it has certainly played an important part in my life.

I also developed paranoia that all the people around me were plotting to steal from me or take my money. I drove people away from me with this behaviour and ended up lonely.

Only a few members of family and friends could bear to be around me and tolerate my constant accusations. I didn't care though, because the only thing that mattered to me was my shopping and the only people I needed were those willing to work for me. After forty six years, and no longer feeling the buzz that I used to, all I had now was the feeling of how soon until I returned to prison. When I stopped, it was fucking hard. The hardest thing I have had to face yet, and I have been through some shit - believe me.

Chapter 8 - Tools of the Trade

I had so many tricks, a list the length of my arm. I was constantly updating my tactics in order to keep my game up-to-date, and to coincide with new alarm systems. In the early days, we operated in gangs and would take bin liners from the stock rooms while someone else distracted the staff. We also used to overpower the alarm system using rape alarms, performed stage fights in a shop - anything to cause a distraction. This was only to set the alarms off after having purchased something relatively small.

I did many bizarre things too. For instance, I had a massive order for leather jackets and they were all alarmed. Together, with an accomplice, we would fill an entire grannies shopping trolley and could usually fit between ten to fifteen jackets, depending on the thickness of the leather. I would then pick up two tops, one navy blue the other black and hold them towards the light therefore triggering the alarm at the precise moment my accomplice wheeled out the jackets. The assistant would think I had triggered the alarm and assume I was merely colour blind.

This carried on for a while. At some point, we began throwing the bags over the alarm systems and eventually, I took to carrying top quality nail clippers and plyers to remove the alarms individually. There was a certain knack doing that without damaging the merchandise. Usually, the alarms are placed on the seam so if a slight rip does appear, you can easily sew it up.

Another method was to actually buy a leather jacket, but before paying for it, I'd put another alarm inside the jacket pocket so as I leave the shop with my purchase again, triggering the alarm, it gives my accomplice time to escape with fifteen other jackets. Then the following day, I would return the jacket for a full refund.

I then graduated my tactics to taking the stores' empty logo bags, covering them with tin foil. Blending with the crowd, in and out rapidly. I even knew where every single street camera was, so to avoid being picked up by them. The more brazen you were, the more you could just get away with things. I remember going into a toy shop one day and I wanted a Mr Man chair for my two-year-old son. As I picked it up, I put it on display above the pram and walked past the till.

If I wanted a pram or pushchair, I'd take a small child with me, cut the alarms then put the kid in the one I desired, wheeling them out of the exit, job done. Smiling as you went passed security.

I also took spare sets of clothes so that if I was spotted, and security guards were looking for me, I changed into different colours. They were looking for a lady in a black jacket and I was now wearing a red one. I would enter the changing rooms of stores wearing baggy clothes, allowing myself to put a new outfit on underneath. Top the outfit off with a nice, new coat then exit wearing the stolen clothes.

I noticed the more brazen I was, the less people seemed to notice. When my son was older and wanted a new tracksuit, I would make him dress in an old one but the same colour as the new one he wanted. We would enter JD Sports and he would put on the new one over the old one whilst I removed the tags.

With my brain so obsessed with shoplifting, I found it hard to switch off. I was forever imagining new ways to scam the shops and use new tools, take advantage of new shops to steal from or new items to add to Kimmy's catalogue. I failed to notice that it was affecting every aspect of my life and interfered with every serious relationship I had. Jay was my boyfriend number five. Before then, I had a few flings - even a couple of one night stands. I never really enjoyed them. I'd often feel empty the next day.

Meaningless sex is just that to me, meaningless. I do not see the point. I like to commit to one person and when I do, I tend to mother them a bit which pissed some of them off.

I am quite old fashioned and a feminist's nightmare. I do everything for my men. I like to spoil them. I love to cook proper food for them, wash and iron all their clothes. My washing was always up-to-date. One boyfriend used to joke that he takes his pants off to have a bath and by the time he gets out, the dirty pants were clean and back in his drawer.

And my house was always immaculate. Dad always used to say, "You can eat yer dinner off Kim's floor." I shower twice a day and will not tolerate mess. I have OCD and recently broke my wrist climbing on the worktop to clean the top of the kitchen cupboards. I am outspoken, but I also dislike arguing. I do not see the point with words. I have been violent in the past. I would lash out with my fists which are still pretty powerful for a petite lady. My days of being "The Boss" and looking after my siblings remains part of me. I never consider the consequences of my actions either. Anyway, I am rambling on a bit now so we shall return to me talking about my four relationships. I had children with all four. You have already heard about Gary and Jim, so my

next chapter shall be dedicated to number three
- Matt Brown.

Chapter 9 - Matt Brown

I was first introduced to Matt by Tammy. We hit it off and became lovers. Matt was quite a nice character but he was a bit of a Mummy's boy, and threw childish tantrums which I could not stand. He worked as a painter and decorator with his Dad, but when there was no work available, I would make him come shopping with me. I had a great relationship with his family and even moved into the family home when we first got together. Janet, his Mum, was battling with her weight so I devised a diet for her and cooked her meals. She soon slimmed down and looked fantastic. I also stuck pictures of huge overweight women on her fridge to deter her from midnight snacks and it must have worked.

Matt and I were together for a while when I received my first small prison sentence into our relationship. Yet again, I was sent to Holloway. It was while I was there I found out that I was pregnant with our child. I also was suffering from severe pains. None of the medical staff believed I was in that much pain. Worst still, they did not believe that I was pregnant. I had to create hell to get myself admitted to hospital where they confirmed that I had chronic appendicitis and operated on me. Afterwards, they sent me to my old stomping ground, East Sutton Park. This time, I was not running, my "Papillion" days were long gone.

A few months later, I had home leave and I made a wager with the other girls that I was not going back and would finish my sentence at home. I went to the doctors and faked a chronic back pain. Knowing that, because I was pregnant, they could not give me an X-ray. The doctors confirmed my illness and wrote me a sick note stating that I was too ill to return to prison. I managed to stay home for six weeks, until one day, the telephone rang and it was the prison warden.

"Kim, get your arse back here now or I shall be sending the police around first thing in the morning." Then he hung up.

I went back and the cheeky bastards shipped me to Holloway for my remaining sentence. I was gutted! Anyway, after being released, I gave birth to my beautiful daughter Georgina. Things were good for a while. Back in those days, we used to party four nights a week with Sunday being the rest day. On Sundays, I would pop out to do a bit of shopping and always cooked a big fat roast dinner. More days than others, we had guests for dinner. I loved to cook, and I still do. I often prepared the dinner and go out for a couple of hours while it was cooking then back home for dinner.

When we did party, I used to drink alcohol and occasionally take a few drugs, purely sociable - then dance the nights away. I used to love dancing and was so active, I never needed the gymnasium. Reflecting back, we hung around in groups, always laughing and up to mischief. Matt was a diabetic so he needed to watch the alcohol intake. After Georgina was born, I became sick of Kingston and being surrounded by fake friends. I wanted to move further afield. Just far enough to be away from the local dramas. We were given temporary housing in Whitton. I got rid of all the haters wrapped around me. The equivalent of nowadays cleaning up your Facebook account, and I deleted loads from my life - even family.

Matt and I loved to party. Even after I spent the entire day shoplifting, I would return home, cook a slap up meal, shower then put my gladrags on for a night in the town. Our weekend used to begin on Wednesday. I used to hang out with Matt and all his laddish mates. I've always had better relationships with men than woman. I think woman used to feel threatened and intimidated by me, mainly due to my loud personality. There was a lot of bitchiness amongst the girls too because I used to wear pretty outrageous outfits. Damn, I had the figure for it so why not?

I loved to receive attention and by God, I got it wearing my leather outfits, leather shorts, thigh high leather boots or very short skirts leather basks. I drew the men towards me, not because I wanted loads of men but because once they were in my clutches, the banter would begin and we would generally end up having a real laugh. Matt never got jealous. He knew I liked to wind them all up. I loved being the centre of attention.

I used to dance all night long. I never went out to sit in a corner. I was there to dance - never to dance for other people but to dance for myself, so we partied hard. On Thursday nights, we went to Options Nightclub in Kingston. I was the queen there and never had to queue because all the bouncers knew and loved me. They'd let me walk in like a VIP. Back then, people used to say I resembled Julia Roberts. Not now but hey, back in the day.

Friday nights used to consist of going to The Astoria or Ministry of Sound, and during the actual weekends, I'd return to Options. On Sunday, we all met up lunchtime at our local pub to discuss the weekly shenanigans. Of course, in between, I still went shopping. Even when I was hanging, someone had to pay for our nights out!

No matter which club I went to, I always wore something outrageous. One night, my friends and I were dressed the same - in micro shorts, stockings and visible suspenders and Timberland boots, and we were mistaken for hired dancers. In the words of Tina Turner, "Private dancer, a dancer for money." No, I was just on a night out and could not stop dancing, not that type of dancing. I guess, because I always had to blend in with the crowd during the day shopping, I liked to stand out at night.

I met a few famous people in the club scene. Kelvin from Eastenders, Neneh Cherry and EMF - although I kept calling them MFL, and kept them entertained. They must have enjoyed my company because a few days later, they called me and asked me to be a Groupie - but I declined.

By this point, Damon and Jade were teenagers and Maggie had recently separated from Dad. I was spending a lot of time at their house with the children. Dad had kidney failure and was finding it hard to cope with the two elder children. So, I gave all three children the option of living with me. Ricky chose to stay with his Grandad, but Damon and Jade joined me for a new life with their Mum. Matt and I were together for four years but the children moving in clearly put a lot of pressure on our relationship. Over something silly, we basically separated. Damon and Matt were both playing Saga game on the PlayStation, Damon won but Matt didn't like that Damon was taunting him. He actually turned very nasty on my son and put his hands around Damon's throat. Well, that was me like a bull to a red flag. You've never seen me move so fast. I did what any normal mother would do. I punched him down the stairs. He went one way and his glasses went the other, and that what the end of yet another relationship.

We remained friends for the sake of our daughter and after we separated, I chose to keep Georgina with me. For the first time in my life, I felt mature enough to offer my kids a good home, so Georgie visited Dad and Nanny at weekends. A few years later, I was sentenced yet again and while I was in prison, Janet my mother-in-law with whom I always assumed I had a close relationship with, filed for custody order of her grandchild. I was heartbroken and what hurt me more was the fact that she didn't have the balls to talk to me about it beforehand. I always trusted and admired her and here she was, acting sneaky behind my back. She even used the tape of me talking about shoplifting on The Kilroy Show in court. I felt like I had been laying on the floor then bang, Janet kicks me in the gut. She maintained it was for Georgina's best interest. Well, Janet did her best, but Georgina seemed to struggle in life a lot more than my other children.

Not only did I have to contend with a custody battle but I had other issues going on the outside that I knew nothing about until my release. I had been given a permanent three bedroom house in a quiet road in Teddington. There were just a small cluster of brand new houses from the Housing Association. A lovely house with a small garden, I had spent the last two years decorating and furnishing it and although it still wasn't exactly how I wanted, it was cosy and clean. Well, when I went into prison, I had asked my step-sister Kate, who I had become recently close to, (she just had her first baby) if she could take care of Damon and Jade while I was away. It was all arranged properly through my social worker and she agreed. She tried her best, but the children had spiralled out of control and were not taking any notice of her. Like their mother, they were super rebellious and she couldn't do it anymore. She was a new mother and a single mother. The stress was too much. All was not lost because Tammy stepped in to save the day. I remember feeling truly grateful that Tammy was there, thus preventing the children going into the foster system or separated.

This gratefulness soon disappeared the minute I was released from prison. Tammy had gone into hiding, underground and abandoned my beautiful home, allowing family members and their friends to trash it. The state of the place, it was ruined. Not one stitch of clothing remained. Even all my underwear disappeared. What furniture had not been stolen was broken. They even stubbed out their cigarettes on the coffee table top. The oven was burnt out. There was ketchup up the walls, Kinder egg toys everywhere. I am not talking just one room trashed. It was every room, and every room was littered with piles of rubbish. Those who did this were pure animals – no, that is an insult to animals. Animals would have left it cleaner.

What sort of a person abandons their responsibilities like that? It still baffles me to this day. I was devastated at the state of the place and had to stay at a friend's house until I had the desire to return. It took me an entire week just to get the place clean and remove all the rubbish. Alright, I may be a thief (well was), but I could never trash somebodies home nor steal all their belongings. It's the worse way to disrespect them.

Tammy had a beautiful home to stay in when she, herself, was homeless and that is how she repaid me. She needed to stay hidden because if I had seen her, I would have battered her and she knew that. Jerry had seen the devastation and that was why he had personally collected me from prison, to soften the blow so to speak.

With hindsight, I should have learned from an earlier lesson. When I was released from Borstal and returned to the family home, everyone rifled through all my belongings and stole all my clothes and personal things. If you cannot trust your own family, then who can you trust? After these types of incidents, I began to distance myself from certain family members. Throughout my life, I had always been the giver and yet all they seemed to do was take from me. Like it was their birth right! I felt that my love for them - and yes I still do carry feelings for them – was never reciprocated. I choose to hang onto my happy childhood memories when we were all laughing together, when we didn't have much but what we did have, we shared. Not just laughter but there was tears too. I do forgive but sometimes, I find it difficult to forget.

Chapter 10 – Mum

I was having a drink in The Cambridge Arms one Thursday night. We were all having a laugh when my phone rang. It was Sylvia. The noise inside the pub was deafening so I took the call outside. "'Ello," I answered.

"Kim it's me," replied Sylvia. "Mum is in a bad way. She's been rushed to hospital and I think you better come." Her voice sounded strained.

"What, what's up wiv 'er?"

"Just make your way to Broadstairs. She's in hospital there,"

"What's she doing there?" I asked.

"She was visiting Tracy. She lives there. When she took a turn for the worse, I'll text you the details where she is OK, and see ya there." Then she hung up. Shit, it must be bad if she phoned me, I thought. I hadn't seen many of the family for years - including Mum. So I got a friend to drive me down there and we arrived in two hours.

When I arrived at the hospital, Tracy was there to greet me and took me to Intensive Care where Mum was. Her emphysema had gotten so bad that she was now using a wheelchair and she must have known that her life was ending because she had planned to visit us all, but sadly never made it. Some were surprised to see I had a nose stud on one side of my nose and a ring on the other, but I was too consumed in my shock when I saw Mum. She could no longer breathe on her own and had a huge hole in her throat. She looked at me. I saw the fear in her eyes and that scared me. I wanted to scream and cry out, why oh why? I knew she was dying, and I think she did too. Inside my head, I was screaming and in pain but I was the eldest and had to hold it together for my siblings. That would have been what Mum wanted. I had to take control and look after them all, just like I did when we were children.

Tammy was sitting there and looked like a little doll. I hadn't seen her since she abandoned my home. Inside, I still wanted to punch her lights out but now it seemed irrelevant and I had to be the bigger person and move past it so I hugged her. I greeted all my siblings then went to the foot of Mum's bed and I tickled her toes. She couldn't speak, so she had been given a children's speak-and-spell toy so she could spell out her words. Mum looked up at me with a big smile then her tears began to flow so I had to use all my strength not to start crying myself. She began to type, spelling, "You look like a pig with that ring in your nose."

"Ha ha Mum, but you always liked little piggies," I replied.

I hadn't seem Mum for more than five years. The others were all around her all the time, so for me it was a shock to see her struggling to breathe and unable to talk. Some of us were crying. I made an excuse that I needed the toilet and exited the room and found the quiet room. Tracy followed me, "Where ya goin'?" she asked

"I'm gonna meditate. It helps me clear my mind."

So I sat in the room and began to chant. I was introduced to Buddhism whilst in prison and found chanting helped me in moments of stress. Then, I had a coffee and returned to sit with Mum. Others left to go and get changed or take a break while Sylvia and I remained overnight. We didn't leave Mum's side as we were too scared, in case she left us. Sylvia and I stayed up most of the night chatting about what will happen when Mum leaves us to go to a better place. It was all very morbid, but it helped us.

The following day, Sylvia and I both needed to return home to get bathed and clean clothes but neither of us wanted to leave Mum. It was heart wrenching but eventually we decided that we had to go and would return straight away. The nightmare was that she was all the way down in Kent so the journey took ages.

On our way back to the hospital, we received the news that Mum had died peacefully. I couldn't really take it in. This wasn't possible. This was Mum, the woman that was invincible. She had given birth to nine children without any drugs and was always our rock as children. She could not have gone, and it wasn't possible. My mind couldn't absorb the information. I guess I was in denial but I had to act strong for the others. I was the eldest.

When we arrived back at the hospital, the nurses had laid Mum out in a beautiful red gown. She did look peaceful. My siblings were all around her, each consumed in their grief. All you could hear was quiet sobbing and sniffles. I chose to stay out of the room and placed my face on the window looking in on all of them. I felt numb inside and also preoccupied that I now had the task of consoling all my siblings. I had to make sure that each and every one of them now had me to help them in their grief. I tried to console some but they pushed me away.

As we all left the hospital, we all made arrangements to meet up at Sylvia's house in a few days to discuss the funeral arrangements. When I arrived home, the house seemed empty.

I was still in shock and hadn't really taken in what had just happened. The house felt dead. Everything seemed dead because I was now without Mum. I hadn't spent much time with her, but I always knew that if I ever needed her she was there. Now the reality was that she was no longer there, and never would be ever again. To end that night, I needed to do something to escape - I ran a bath. I always feel better when I'm clean. Once dry and dressed, I did the typical British thing and made a strong cup of tea. I don't usually take sugar but I made it sweet because I knew that was good for shock, then I went into bed.

It was winter time, yet there was a wasp flying around my bedroom. My mind started to wonder, why was there a wasp there right now? Weird, Mum was allergic to wasps and hated it if one flew near her. She was also allergic to pork and strawberries. They made her break out in blotches. I couldn't sleep because my phone was constantly ringing for various reasons. This time, Sylvia called. She was devastated and needed someone to talk to. I remember her words vividly. She said, "I can't believe I'm never gonna see Mum again. To talk to her, hug her, kiss her!" She was sobbing down the phone.

"I know, Slyv," I replied. "But ya just gotta think, she's in a better place now. She is watching over you. Watching over us all."

I tried to give her words of comfort, but there are never any words to ease someone when they have so much grief in their heart, especially when it's your Mum. Your Mum is not only your Mum, she is your best friend. The woman you bonded with and the woman you trusted one hundred percent. You know that she is the most important woman in your life and she would die for her children.

Loss is part of animal instinct that's in us all, yet I'd always struggled to find words describing the death of my Mum. Even as I write this, the feelings that I buried all those years ago are stirring, because I chose to be the strong one - to keep it together for the others' sake. After the phone call with Sylvia, I didn't say much. I just gave her my listening ear because I knew that it was what she needed. I do recall saying that I would go out shopping and get everyone new outfits for the funeral. That was, I thought, a way to cheer them all up. I drifted into a deep sleep with the wasp still circling around my ceiling light.

When I awoke the following day, something unexplainable happened. I could not get up from the bed. It was as though an invisible force had me pinned down. I tried to scream but no sounds came out of my mouth. I struggled again. I felt drained. It must have lasted a few minutes which felt longer. Then, finally, I managed to get up. It was then I heard Mum's voice, "No shopping, Kim."

What the fuck was that?

Had I imagined it? Her voice was so vivid, that I burst into tears. Come on Kim, get a grip, I told myself. I went downstairs and made myself some tea and toast, but that was a waste of time because I had no appetite. I then proceeded to bathe and was getting ready to hit the shops for everyone's new outfits then drove into Kingston with a fellow shopper. As I got out of the car, something overwhelmed me and I had a mini breakdown on the spot and began to weep. I couldn't shop in that frame of mind so I had to abort mission and I rang Sylvia. This time, I was sobbing.

"I can't get the outfits. I can't shop. So sorry, I dunno what's wrong with me." I blurted in between sniffles.

"Don't do it," Sylvia said. "Get in the car and come 'ere to me." So I did. I drove to Sylvia's house. As I made my way there, I pulled myself together and told myself, "No more crying." I knew Mum had stopped me shopping that day and I had to respect her wishes.

I arrived at Sylvia's and her daughter Julia and my sister Tracy were already there. We drank coffee and they gave me words of comfort. We began reminiscing about our childhood and recalling funny stories, some of which I had forgotten. I was normally in most of them being the black sheep, or the nutty one.

Sylvia had spoken to Patrick and Michael about Mum's passing. Michael was particularly in a bad way and had trouble accepting it. He was the baby of the family and still lived at home. Mum doted on Michael. He was her baby. The others thought he was a spoiled brat, but now I have my Paris, I can relate to why she spoiled him so much. Your last child is the one you put everything into because there are no more siblings that follow to take up your time. It makes sense.

I will never forget the look in Michael's eyes. It was heart breaking. I don't think he ever fully recovered from losing Mum. He lost both his parents by losing her because he didn't really see much of Dad. Seeing Michael crumbling before my eyes tore me apart. Although I tried in vain to comfort him with words, there is nothing you could do to help others with their grief because we all deal with it in different ways. Some of us recover and others never quite get there.

At the funeral, I made a point of saying that we should all keep in touch and not reunite just when sad things occur. They all seemed to lavish me with attention, and I did try to stay in touch. But gradually, we all drifted apart again as we returned to our busy lives. The funeral was held in Basingstoke and the only one out of us siblings that had any money was Patrick. He was calling the shots as far as the arrangements went. After all, he was paying for it. I made sure that Mum got her glass carriage. She told me years earlier that she always wanted to get married in one. It was evident that her own mother must have read her way too many fairy tales when she was a child.

Dad attended the funeral too. He was sad that day. I think he was sadder because he could see all of his children hurting and felt powerless to help us. Although Dad loved Maggie, he never stopped loving Mum. Mum remarried a man named Frank. Frank was alright, but a bit annoying. He would start to rant and lecture us about everything.

The church service was lovely and Scott rose to the pulpit and read out a beautiful poem called "Footsteps". As I listened to Scott reading, I couldn't help but notice that he had aged over the last few years and he seemed to resemble Rigsby from the television programme Rising

Damp. I chuckled inside. The service finished to a ballad by Barry Manilow - my Mum's favourite. After church, we all went outside where they lowered Mum's coffin and we all threw a rose on top of it. I kissed my rose and screamed, "Love ya, Mum". There were tears streaming down all of our faces.

On the way out of the cemetery, Frank stood at the entrance and shook everyone's hand whilst thanking them for coming. I looked at Dad and started to panic inside. I knew my Dad. If Frank said to him, "Thank you for coming", Dad was likely to kick off. Sure enough, that was more or less what happened. Dad tried to pass Frank without shaking his hand but Frank grabbed it and said, "Thank you for coming". With that, Dad rapidly withdrew his hand and started shouting.

"Thank you for coming? You prick. I've got more rights to be 'ere than you, arse 'ole."

I ran and grabbed Dad, trying to diffuse the situation. "Dad, not now come on," and I led him away. He wanted to punch Frank.

My Mum's sister Patricia was there - my Aunty Patricia. She only lived in Raynes Park, not far from us, but we were rarely in contact. Throughout our childhood, she scarcely visited us. At least she had made the effort. "Your Mum would be extremely proud of all of you," she said. We all made sure that she had a beautiful send off and the flowers were gorgeous.

I cooked and prepared all the food for the wake. It was held at Robbie's house in Basingstoke. The vicar was there too and I decided to liven up the party. I flashed my boobs at the vicar. Everyone began to giggle. "Ha ha, you are funny, Kim," said Aunty Patricia. I loved to see everyone stuffing their faces and complimenting my food. Later, reality set in and we all returned to our lives. Life goes on, the circle of life!

Chapter 11 - Scott

Scott spent a brief time living with me in my house in Teddington. He was in a bit of a drifting period of his life and needed somewhere to stay. I suggested he stayed with me for a while just until he was back on his feet.

Typical Farry style, Scott had a brainwave as to how we could make some money on a project he had thought of. We needed to buy an old banger car, get a new engine, hire a mechanic to do it all up, and then sell it for twice the money we paid for it. Well, I didn't even have to think about it. If it meant profit, I was in. So I shelled out six hundred pounds and he bought the old banger and a new engine, booked it into the garage to them to carry out the repairs.

Four weeks had passed and there was still no car. Every time I asked Scott what was happening with the car, he made some excuse and by then I was beginning to get suspicious. I knew he had gambling problems in the past thanks to Dad introducing him to that world at an early age. I suspected he went back to old habits so I became Inspector Gadget or Sherlock Holmes and investigated. I got hold of the phone bill and rang every number on it that I didn't recognise. I found the number for the garage where the car was.

"Yeah, we've got the car," said the man on the other end of the phone. "It's been ready for six weeks. Just waiting on the payment, and then you can 'av it."

I saw red. The little bastard had been given the money for the car weeks ago. I paid it and trusted him, yet he had gambled the money away. I waited until he returned home. I was fuming. He walked in, happy as Larry with not a care in the world.

"You lying little shit!" I said to him.

"What, what ya talking about?"

"You fuckin' know, the money, the car." I grabbed him and threw him up against the hallway wall.

"Stop fucking lying, Scott."

"Okay, you've got me bang to rights. I confess. I didn't mean to lose it. I thought I was on a winning streak."

Eventually both calm, we sat down and discussed his problems and resolved the situation. We cut our losses and basically I lost money, listening to his quick fix money-making skills. I had just learnt yet another valuable lesson in life. Don't trust Scott with money. I wasn't cut out to be in the car dealing industry. I needed to stick to what I knew, which was my shopping empire. It was a far cleaner and easier way to earn my money. Ha ha ha, I'm chuckling to myself when he realised that Sherlock Holmes had out smarted him. He shat himself.

Chapter 12 - Mental

Prior to one of my most recent sentences, I knew I was due a short vacation from Her Majesty's Service. For once, I wasn't quite ready to go. I had a few things to sort out. My first priority was to get support needed for the children. I needed a bit of extra time to myself so I came up with a plan. It was a mental plan and I mean that literally. I admitted myself to hospital. I made Kate come with me to the emergency unit at West Middlesex Hospital and asked her to tell them that she was worried for my welfare and didn't believe it was safe for me to be at home around my children for fear that I may harm them or myself because, lately, I was very aggressive.

Once again, I put on my acting cap. I am like Worzel Gummidge. I managed to convince the doctors I needed to be assessed mentally and then admit me. First, they tested me to see if I was severely depressed and whether I was a kleptomaniac. I mentioned that I smoked weed every night so they gave me a tiny little purple pill that made me feel stoned. They sent me into the mental ward of a hospital.

Jesus, it was definitely "One Flew Over the Cuckoo's Nest" in there.

The nurses showed me around and settled me into my own small room. I left my belongings on top of the bed while the nurse took me away to see the doctor for an assessment. Upon my return, I noticed another male patient wearing a girl's coat which made me stare a little. I soon realised it was my own coat. It was a bit like a déjà vu from my early prison days. I confronted him. "Oi mate, that's my coat. What ya doin'? I wannit back."

He had the cheek to look at me like I was a nutter. I kid you not, he freaked me out a bit so I told the nurse and she got my coat back. Needless to say I never wore it again, fuck that! I found out he was a serial kleptomaniac, how ironic! I wanted a kleptomaniac ticket because to me, it was a get out of jail free card. The police just informed your doctor and you wouldn't be charged.

After a few days, I could no longer stand it. It wasn't because I was there, but the fact that the staff did nothing with the patients other than dose them up on medication. They even served us tea and coffee in filthy unwashed cups. I am telling you, I have always been a little mental but I was the only normal one there. A patient would kick off screaming and was then dragged away. I felt like I was in a film.

After my initial assessment with the doctor, they did nothing with me other than prescribe drugs. Nobody spoke to me. No other treatments were offered. I tried to converse with some of the patients. Some could hold a conversation, others were on planet gaga. I actually felt disgusted that these human beings were being neglected and cared for in such a sluggish manner. So me being me, one night I decided to cheer them all up. We were all gathered around the television watching Top of the Pops. I started to dance and shouted, "Come on everyone, up yer get, let's dance woo hooo." Woops, I caused a real commotion. It was funny. They all got up dancing and were all having fun but some were clearly too overexcited. We were all up on the tables dancing. Well, at least I was. One poor man wet himself with excitement.

This got me into severe trouble and I was thrown out that night. These people needed fun in their lives. Most were severely depressed and nothing was done to improve their quality of life. They just get shut away from reality and dosed up on medication. I still think it is disgusting. Surely, lifting their spirits was the way forward?

I was there for two weeks and not issued a kleptomaniac card. One guy in particular, Thomas, had latched onto me. He suffered from severe depression and came for a decent home.

Yet, family paid to have him stay there rather than be treated elsewhere. We remained friends and he even visited my home. One minute we would engage in a decent conversation and I would think, wow what an intelligent young man. Then the next minute, I could not make head or tail of what he was talking about. He brought round his heavy metal music to listen to at my house. I have to say, it's not my preference at all but I tolerated it. He visited a few times then I never saw him again. However, that may have been because I was back in prison.

Chapter 13 - Back to East Sutton Park again

I cannot knock this prison. Compared to Holloway, it is like the Hilton Hotel. They even had a working farm! Over the years, I suppose it became my second home. A retreat where I could rest and recuperate, mentally and physically. I chose to work on the farm – yep, Farmer Kim. Considering I have never really been a super animal lover, this was a bit unusual. But you can't deny my need to spend the day outdoors in the fresh air, away from the mundane prison life. It gave me a sense of freedom. It was an early start - five thirty in the morning starts. You ate your breakfast at the farm and only returned for lunch. It was hard work and I worked with the pigs. Pigs are amazing animals, more intelligent than dogs and each have their own little characters. I called one Wilber. It had to be done! Charlotte's Web inspired me for that name picking. I had my favourites. I spent each day shovelling pig shit and began to enjoy it.

Before I went into prison, my weight had dropped to a size six. I used to wear leggings under jeans to try and appear less skinny. So, the minute I entered prison, other inmates assumed

I was a skinny junkie and became astounded when they realised the truth. I used to smoke weed every night. Nothing heavy, just one joint to help me sleep. But no one could approach me when it took effect because once it hit me, it made me paranoid and aggressive. Anyway, once in prison, I decided it was time to beef myself up and I joined the gymnasium and passed my fitness test. I gained weight and, upon my release, was a size fourteen which was a little too much for me because I am only five foot two.

Lifting pig shit is extremely hard work and it weighed a ton. At first, I struggled with my workload. After a few weeks in the gymnasium, however, I was throwing it into the truck like a burly man. Working on the farm changed my outlook towards animals. I became Farmer of the Year. I would have given Seth out of Emmerdale a run for his money. Not only did I become educated about pigs, I also learnt about cows, goats and rams. It felt like the years I had spent watching Felicity Kendal in "The Good Life" had paid off. Us girls were allowed to go down to the farm whenever we wanted. It was there you got time alone and for a few hours, it felt like you were on a day trip out to the country with the family. I relaxed there. No brain ticking away about shopping, just like being on a health farm.

I loved to draw and illustrate things, but only when I was in prison. If I wrote anyone a letter, the envelope would be ornated with my illustrations. Matt remarked the envelopes were more interesting than my letters. I would decorate them with flowers, cartoon characters or whatever came to my mind at the time. The other inmates admired my work and some got me to draw for them, for a price of course. I would charge stamps or chocolate, anything I needed or was running out of.

During one of my stints at East Sutton Park, the word spread around about my drawing and next thing I knew, I was asked to help create some poster for an upcoming event to be held at the prison. The big celebrity, Esther Rantzen, was arriving for a charity event that we were holding. It was a bit like a school fete with different stalls. I designed the poster and a few others for the stalls. Obviously, to make a bit of money, we were each allowed to invite an outsider to attend but it was forbidden to invite your partners. I was with Jim at the time and I ignored the prison protocol by inviting him. What a funny day that was. Everyone was so preoccupied, fussing around the celebrity that the guards were not paying much attention. I was attending to a stall, but due for my break soon, I signalled to Jim to come over. "Oi, I'm on me break in a minute, wait fer me over there," and I pointed to near the door.

The minute I was relieved of my stall, I ran over to Jim. The place was heaving so we went unnoticed and slipped out the door. I grabbed his hand and we ran towards the farm as fast as we could. Once we were at the farm, all that was there were the animals. We ripped off each other's clothes and had passionate sex there. It was even more exciting because there was the added thrill that we might get caught. And we did get caught. Not by a guard or even another inmate, but by a huge cow that came running towards us. "Quick, fuckin' run," I said.

What a funny sight - we both jumped up with our underwear around our ankles and proceeded to run away from the cow. We could only take little steps because our underwear was restricting our footsteps. How we roared with laughter when we finally felt safe from the cow. Then we just slipped back to the party unnoticed.

During my last stay there, I met a very pretty timid young girl called Debbie. It was her first time in prison and she was not coping very well at all. She sobbed her heart out from the start. She was a sweet and calm girl, with a gentle nature, not the usual type to be in prison and clearly out of place. She had a small daughter who her mother was looking after but she missed her terribly and hadn't even committed a crime, bless her. Her boyfriend was a gangster with connections to The Krays. A parcel was sent to her address with her name on it containing drugs. Customs had picked it up on route which she had no knowledge about and she took the fall for her boyfriend.

There were quite a few girls sentenced for drug-related offences when in fact they were innocent and covering for their boyfriends. I went over and comforted Debbie knowing that if she carried on like that, other inmates would immediately pick up on her weakness and intimidate her making her stay in prison hell.

"Kim, I'm gonna tell 'em the truth that it weren't me but me boyfriend," Debbie said.

"Are you fukin' nuts," I replied. "They'll get yer family. What's done is done mate. You've gotta ride it out and fuckin' pull yerself togeva mate, or some cunt's gonna make yer life 'ell in 'ere." I took her under my wing. Boy did she need it. I even lent her my clothes to wear on visiting days because I had taken some nice outfits with me.

Debbie was being bullied a bit by two other inmates. Why do bullies always hang around in packs? I caught her sobbing in the dormitory one day and asked her what was wrong.

"They won't leave me alone. They keep threatening me and I áin't don nofin to 'em?" she said.

"Who, that blonde bitch Jenny an' 'er mates?"

"Yeah Kim, but I don't want any trouble."

"You won't get any mate. Now, get a grip and forget about it and for fucks sake. Stop fuckin' crying, you can't cry in 'ere!"

I waited for my revenge until we went to beauty classes (yes, we even had beauty classes). The blonde one started being bitchy towards Debbie. Just any excuse to belittle her or make a nasty comment. Once I had heard enough, that was it. The little bell went off in my head and I jumped right into Jenny's face. I moved up close so our noses were practically touching. Then, in a slow but menacing voice said, "Leave her the fuck alone, it's 'ard enough in 'ere without cunts like you giving 'er shit. Carry on love and you've got me to deal with, you fuckin' mug."

Jenny looked a bit sheepish but didn't say a word. After that, they left Debbie alone. Debbie relayed her experiences to her boyfriend who thanked me for looking after her and promised to repay me once I was released. He wanted to meet up with me but he was a big time gangster and, quite rightly, my Dad advised me against the idea so I never did. I was just a small time shoplifter and preferred to stay that way. By the time I was released, Debbie sorted herself out and stood up to the bullies who left her alone.

Chapter 14 - Prison Food

You would think that prison food would be standard issue. I pictured it to be the same all over the country - a bit like school dinners. It wasn't and it varied widely, depending on the prison.

Holloway food was revolting. I actually chose to go vegetarian there because their menu was better than the meat options. Breakfast consisted of porridge or boiled eggs, (ha ha, that just made me think of Ronnie Barker in Porridge). Lunch would be some type of sandwich, and then dinner was some kind of mushed up food with mash that smelt like dog food. The smell made me heave and I couldn't eat it. Pudding was generally some type of rock cake that you could break your teeth with. Come to think of it, that was pretty dangerous to serve in prison because I am sure it could have been used as a deadly weapon. Thank fuck my visits to Holloway were always temporary or I could have died from starvation or dog food poisoning.

Bullwood Hall served pretty much the same shit as Holloway. Breakfast was rubber eggs, dried up bacon, cold toast and the rest was mainly stodgy food. It felt as if the cooks were attempting to fatten us up, as there was nothing healthy served whatsoever. I resorted to buying noodles and tuna from the canteen instead of a totally unhealthy diet.

Then my favourite, East Sutton Park. The food was cooked from scratch. You could tell everything was home cooked and the chefs used fresh ingredients. If I didn't know better, I could have sworn Gordon Ramsay was the head chef. We ate toast, porridge, cereal, boiled eggs and fresh milk. Lunch consisted of a choice (yes, you actually chose like as you would in a restaurant) of hot or cold food. One day, I'd have a nice, fresh chicken salad or a pasta dish the next. For the evening meal, there was always something tasty like Jerk chicken, rice and peas - always a healthy combination. And the grand finale, on Sunday's, was a lovely roast dinner followed by delicious pudding, sponge cake and custard.

Upon my release from my last stay at East Sutton Park the governor called me to her office.

"Now Kim, you have been here five times now and although I wish you all the best on the outside, I am telling you now that if you reoffend and are sentenced to a prison stay again, I will refuse to have you here because you clearly like it too much."

"Don't worry, I'm not coming back," I said.

Chapter 15 - Bullies

There is nothing I hate more than a bully, so imagine how I felt when I found out that my daughter Jade, as a teenage girl, was being bullied by an older girl at school. There was a gang of them but, as always, one was the ring leader. I was lucky that she didn't bottle it inside, but as soon as she felt threatened, she came to me and confided in me. I know some children are terrified to do that.

We were all living in Whitton at the time and I knew Jade was no angel. She was a bit of a tearaway but that still did not justify her being bullied. The older girls in question resented her because she was a stunning looking girl and all the boys at school loved Jade. Like mother, like daughter! The irony of it is that she had no remote interest in dating. I received a telephone call from the headmistress that Jade was "having problems" as she put it. We arranged a meeting but nothing was resolved and the girls continued to make Jade's life hell. The bullying continued. After the second phone call, I decided to take matters into my own hands and devised a little plan. Oh yes, I was going to sort this out once and for all. No one fucks with my daughter.

So being petite, I dressed up in one of Jade's spare school uniforms, drove to the school and arranged for Jade to meet me outside. She then directed me to the PE hall where the ring leader was. She was a lot bigger than me - a big lump I thought. Fuck me, she's big! Then my rage took over. I grabbed her by the scruff of the neck and threw her up against the gymnasium wall and said, "If you ever fuck with my daughter again, I will smash your fuckin' muvver up, understand?"

She was pretty speechless but nodded and then I left. I was reported and subsequently banned from entering the school premises ever again. A few days later, the headmistress unofficially paid me a house visit.

"Ms Farry, I cannot under any circumstances condone your actions the other day. But I can confirm that the bullying at the school has decreased dramatically since then." I remember Dad used to say to me, "The only way to beat a bully is to be a bigger bully." So, watch out, Kimmy's about. The children started to call me psychopath.

Damon had problems at the very same school but this time it wasn't a fellow student giving him grief but an actual teacher. He was twelve or thirteen and the school assignment was called "Pets Day". All the children were encouraged to take their pets to school and do a presentation on them in front of the class. So Damon arrived with his pet tarantula named Rex. In fact, he ended up having five giant spiders and it cured my phobia.

The teacher (maybe he had a phobia) wasn't impressed and began to ridicule Damon in front of the other students making nasty comments. It upset Damon a lot. He didn't say anything to me, but his close friend Liam telephoned me to explain the situation and that Damon was really upset that the teacher had constantly insulted him. I told Liam to meet me outside the school and jumped into the car. Once I arrived, Liam led me to the classroom. I didn't give a flying fuck that I had been banned from the premises. I barged in without knocking, gave the teacher a few chosen words then took Damon and Rex home.

As I said, I don't tolerate bullying. Even a few years earlier to Damon's bullying, I had been shopping in Epsom with Matt. We were driving home in my Mini Metro when I noticed two blonde sisters (yes, you know who you are) had an autistic boy up against the wall. They were being nasty to him. I stopped the car in the middle of the traffic. I didn't care that it was stuffed with stolen merchandise. I ran over to them. I knew the girls from the estate.

"Get you' fuckin' 'ands off 'im," I shouted, while physically dragging them away.

"We weren't doin' nuffin'," said one of the girls.

"Yes you fuckin' were. My eyes don't lie, now fuck off you pair of bullies before I bully you."

They quickly disappeared. I like to think it was through shame but somehow, I doubt it. I drove the young man home, squeezed amongst all my bags in the back of the car. God, I hate bullies.

Chapter 16 - Me

Me being me, I had everyone out shopping and working for me. I can be quite a bossy person, hence why I was given the nickname "The Boss". People came and went throughout my life, just the same as all our lives. I used to tempt them into temptation and lead them into my business venture. I just had to dangle the carrot - which was cash, money, it drove me too. Some were eager to shop with me, others unwilling associates. I truly believed it was the best way to earn money, albeit illegal.

My mind forever ticking over with new ideas and, when I had exhausted some of my new scams, I passed the details onto other shoplifters and commence another new scam. I shared my ideas. I even got Maggie, who worked her arse off and never even got a parking ticket in her life, to come with me one day with a stolen chequebook. That was a disaster.

If I came across anyone struggling financially, I always helped out whether it was clothes, food or even toiletries courtesy of Boots. Mentally too, I am great at solving other people's problem and a great listener. A regular agony aunt if you like. I was just shit at solving my own.

As I said before, there were a lot of people that liked to be around me purely for "things". They did not have my welfare at heart whatsoever. But I am no fool I can read people pretty well and I would soon move on from these people and delete them from my life. The media latched onto the "Robin Hood" comment, but everyone knows how the media like to twist words. I prefer "Father Christmas" or "Mother Christmas" - my favourite time of year, at least it used to be. That's when the shops are bustling with people and the staff are too busy to notice anything.

I have a huge heart and loved to spoil everyone at Christmas time. I tailored every present I stole for the individual. One year, I got Kate a full length beige leather coat with a fur collar. I was trying to liven her up as she was dressing too frumpy for her age. I could see by her face that she wasn't sure when she opened it. She even sent me a text one night during EastEnders saying, "Dot Cotton is wearing my coat." Sure enough, Dot had a fur collared coat on. But nothing like the one I had given Kate. We did giggle. Eventually, after she had worn it out a few times and received compliments on her new coat, she began to love it.

When they – the media - put words into my mouth about "Robin Hood", it was because I was trying to explain that my shoplifting was never just about me, me, me. I am not that sort of person. I merely wished to emphasise that, throughout my illegal career, I loved to share things too. If a friend had just given birth and struggled to make ends meet, I would grab a bag of different aged baby clothes for them, so they get through the first year. We all know how quickly babies grow and how expensive they are. That was my present for the baby.

Also, if I noticed other friend's cupboards were bare or they were eating beans and sausages on a daily basis, I'd get them a large bag of shopping containing treats they wouldn't afford – prawns, a bit of steak, joints of meat and so on. I never visited anyone empty handed. I didn't do it to be praised. I did it because seeing other people's faces light up gave me a buzz too.

I absolutely love tattoos and enjoy the pain of having them done. The pain to me makes it even more worthwhile. There is nothing like getting a tattoo done when I am mentally upset, because it takes my mind from the anguish and am therefore distracted. Piercings, I also adore and have had quite a few over the years. Tattoos are better because, after the pain, you see the rewards with the end results, providing that you have been to a reputable tattoo artist and not chosen a shitty design. I have thirteen tattoos and my favourite has to be my sleeve on my left arm. If anyone wants the name of a good tattoo artist, I highly recommend Jay from Sunbury. He is a master at his profession.

I also love a bit of plastic surgery, and why not? I've had three breast enhancements and would like just one more to get my desired result. I would love to have a few other bits of surgery done but, for me, my boobs are very important. After having children, for us women, our bodies change. Well, mine did, that is for sure. Nobody wants to look in the mirror and see two saddle bags hanging down or hanging flower pots. I didn't, so I chose to improve myself with surgery and regain my confidence as a woman.

Living with Jim and his obsession with page three models probably didn't help. All the fried egg jokes did knock my confidence. Men like boobs and bums which sadly, whether we like it or not, both sag with age. No, I am not thinking about having surgery on my bottom. I have chosen exercise for that and pound those buttocks on a daily basis. I now workout daily and eat healthy food. I always had small boobs but now I am the proud owner of a pair of 34Es. After my last boob operation, I bumped into a friend in Kingston who went back saying, "I kid you not, I only bumped into Kim Farry today shopping and she looked like fucking Dolly

Parton." Others refer to me as "Jordan", but I do not base my look on anyone. It is just the way I want to look - the Kim Farry look.

I love to help people and not just with stolen goods - with a listening ear and even care for elderly people. One day, an old man was struggling carrying his shopping. He was gasping for breath, so I stopped him.

"Excuse me, d'you need a hand?" I said.

You could see he was a very proud man and about to refuse my help but I insisted.

"Give us yer bags and I will carry em. Where d'you live?"

He told me where and we walked together while I carried his bags and made a little small talk. I am not great at small talk but I did my best. When we arrived, I gave him my number and said if he needed any help shopping or anything else to call me. He never did. He had probably seen me on Kilroy and thought, thieving little bastard, ha ha.

I love the Carry On films and quite fancy reprising Barbara Windsor's role in "Carry on Camping" with my bra smacking someone in the face. I loved James Cagney films, especially "Angels With Dirty Faces" where his character is a hard man but has to pretend he is not to deter the youngsters from following in his footsteps. I collect Betty Boop items and teddy bears, but

China ones. Betty Boop interested me from my younger days and my current boyfriend, Jay, sometimes teases me saying I am her double and we look like twins, ha ha.

I also have a fascination with Marilyn Monroe. My famous motto in keeping hold of a man is the famous Jerry Hall quote, "To keep a man, you must be a maid in the living room, a cook in the kitchen and a whore in the bedroom." I am good at these, or so I have been told. I like to dress up for my men in nice underwear and never suffer from hairy leg or hairy armpit days. I never neglect how I look, even in the winter. I always like to look and feel sexy. In all my relationships, I made an effort in the bedroom and like to dress up in sexy and kinky outfits and believe the way to a man's heart is through his stomach and then dessert which is meeeee, ha ha. I am pretty much OCD about everything in my life, personal hygiene, grooming, housework – always needed these sorted one hundred percent.

Whenever I feel down in the dumps and blue, I always faced it alone and would never burden other people. I hide myself away until that feeling passed. I believe, well personally for me, I recover quicker that way.

My infectious laugh embarrasses many of my friends and family. I have tried to control it, but I just can't. My son Jimmy, my boyfriend Jay and even my best friend Michelle - they all cringe and run away when I start to laugh in public, especially if we are in some official place. They leave me so fast that, when I look around, I look like a complete nutter standing there alone cackling to myself. Not a good look!

Ironically enough, I am great with children, just not my own. They seem to relate to me probably because I revert to doing crazy childish things with them. I absolutely dote on my grandson Kyron. When he comes to stay, Nanny spoils him rotten. I grew hard and bitter when I left my own children so slowly but surely, I am losing the barrier I built up and letting them all into my heart.

I love to quote sayings. These are my favourites; "Don't mess with the best cos the best don't mess" ... "The early bird catches the worm" - I have lived my life by that one ... "Don't do to others that you do not like done to yourself." That one is spot on.

I am still passionate about anything and everything I do, and have never done anything by half, be it shoplifting, cleaning, cooking or just beating the living daylights out of somebody. I never bothered to study at school so I will never know if, maybe, my life would have been different. If I had taken a different path in life, we'll never know. All I know is that I became a genius shoplifter. I loved the colour of money, and still do.

I am definitely unique - a one off. There is nobody else on this planet like me. Thank God. I mean, who needs another Kim Farry, fuck that. Somebody stop me, smoking – as I quote from The Mask film!

Chapter 17 - Dave Miller

My final serious relationship, until my current love, was Dave Miller. I first met Dave years ago when he had long hair, then hadn't seen him again until years later in the Cambridge Arms where Dad was a regular. He used to hang around with the Slater family and Sid Riley who I had known for years. We started dating a couple of times a week then after six weeks it became serious and we became lovers.

Dave was handsome, funny, had the body of a Chippindale stripper and a hard worker. He was the first man in my life to actually help in supporting me financially, well, apart from Jerry but that was just a platonic friendship. We spent a good seven years together and had some wonderful times and produced Paris, our beautiful princess. Dave hit it off with everyone and Dad was especially fond of him. Apart from Gary, Dad didn't really take to Jim or Matt but he adored Dave because there really was nothing to dislike about him. He was always polite and a delight to be around. He stood up to me too, which I sometimes needed because I am far from easy to live with.

Ultimately, we complimented each other and things were good. He helped build our three bedroom house in Teddington into a warm and cosy house, whereas my other two palatial homes, I had to do everything alone. Because I spent nearly everyday either visiting or phoning Dad, each Sunday, Dave would collect Dad in his car and bring him to my house for his Sunday dinner. Dad would ring me up asking, "Kim, can't you drive over, 'e scares the shit out of me the way 'e drives?"

"No Dad. You know I ain't got a licence," I would reply.

Dave was not a thief but at one point he wanted to make a fast buck so decided dealing cocaine. At the time, it was the way forward. I was shocked when the police raided my house. It was early evening, we had just eaten dinner. I was washing up and heavily pregnant at the time. Dave was on the toilet. All we heard was a massive bang as they broke the front door down with a battering ram. They were fucking everywhere, police with riot gear on huge shields, police dogs, guns at us from all angles. I kid you not, it was like being a mad film. I was accustomed to police raids but never on this scale. They entered the kitchen shouting.

"Put your hands on your head," they screamed.

It seemed as though there were hundreds of the fuckers everywhere. For fucks sake, I was a shoplifter not a murderer. Someone local had heard Dave was dealing and didn't like the competition so his name was put forward to the police, i.e. someone grassed him up. Somebody had also told the police we were in possession of firearms. I didn't own as much as a water pistol, let alone a gun!

They asked what was in the chest freezer so I replied, "Only a dead body." Their faces were a picture. Dave and I were stripped searched and then arrested. They took Dave to Kingston police station, but I was taken to Richmond where they continued to question me for hours. You know the drill – good cop, bad cop. They found 17 wraps in a coat pocket but I maintained that I had no knowledge of any drugs and that the coat was left behind after a party. Every question, I answered with 'no', then eventually after ten hours, they released me without any charges.

Each of the wraps weighed different amounts so Dave confessed to having a cocaine addiction and was not charged with intent to supply, just for personal use. The police found no wads of cash nor any weighing scales. A few days earlier, I had a bad feeling in my gut and had disposed of them. Dave said the police treated him decently. We believe that the guy, Phil, who came to score some drugs had in fact brought the police with him, at least that's what it looked like. Sadly, he became a heroin addict.

Whilst searching for drugs, they found two thousand five hundred pounds worth of my vouchers that I had been saving up and they confiscated them. They were pretty gutted because the next day, they had to return my vouchers. They knew how I had got them. I knew how I had them, but they could not prove it and the vouchers were not deemed stolen. The goods I had exchanged them for were long gone back in the shops, returned to their rightful owners so there was not a thing the police could do about it. I fucked the system once the shops introduced vouchers because I no longer had a house full of stolen items to sell; they went straight back to the shops.

Chapter 18 – Germany

Upon my final release from prison, Dave's mum had a surprise in store for us both. She booked a romantic holiday for two in Paphos in Cyprus for Dave and me. I know this is going to sound really ungrateful, but I really didn't want to go. Paris was only three months old and I had missed her terribly whilst in prison and wanted to get home with all my home comforts, spending a few weeks cuddling my baby girl. I didn't want to sound ungrateful and Dave seemed excited so I agreed to the holiday and Dave's mum looked after Paris. My gut feeling was not to go, and I went against that feeling. I later discovered to always follow your gut!

So, we are at the airport and headed for the bar where we met an older lady and another couple. We chatted with them and a few laughs while I was knocking back the Jack Daniels at a pretty rapid pace. I really was missing Paris. That was all I could think about, until I heard the plane was delayed. That's it, I thought. It is a sign. I am not going, but no - the flight was eventually opened and so we proceeded to the boarding gates. But, by this time, I was pretty drunk, but hey ho. Dave and I boarded the plane.

On the plane, there were no seats left together so I was at the back and Dave seated a few rows in front of me. Now up in the air, I really needed the toilet so I asked the air steward where the nearest toilet was and he pointed in the direction. As I got out of my seat and began to walk towards it, the steward was behind me. Whether he stumbled and grabbed out to stop himself falling, I will never know. But all of a sudden, he grabbed me from behind and his hands landed on my breasts. I saw red, turned round and punched him in the face. He fell to the floor. I then began ranting and raving until other members of staff arrived to calm me down and sit me back in my seat.

Dave had also drunk plenty of alcohol and during this drama, he was asleep - didn't hear a sound. He slept through it all. Little did I know that, in the meantime, the plane had been diverted to Germany. Once we landed, armed police boarded the plane and escorted Dave and I off where we were arrested. Poor Dave had no idea what was going on as he was awoken from his lovely sleep to armed German police speaking in German, dragging him off the plane. I was shouting abuse and being a typical pain in the arse.

"Speak English mate, yer 'aving a laugh."

I had verbal diarrhoea, which was a waste of time because I am sure they didn't even speak English. They took us both to the police station in separate cars and wow, I have never seen such a clean prison cell. It was so fresh and immaculate, an absolute pleasure to frequent.

We were released the following morning without charge - just banned from entering Germany for life which does not make any sense whatsoever because I was there for punching the steward. I suppose the incident happened while we were in German airspace, therefore it is an offence committed in Germany. That's mad. I mean, how can you say that a country owns a part of the sky. It baffles me.

We had to sign our release then walk miles with our bags back to the airport. When we arrived to the airport, no one seemed very helpful about how we were to go about getting home. No one gave us any useful information. The police were still following us. I was tired and hungry, eventually losing my temper, shouting abuse at them.

"Kim will you fuckin' be'ave. They'll probably shoot us," Dave shouted at me.

We finally met another traveller who was on his way home to England from France and he helped us book our return flights. We had to pay another eight hundred pounds to get home, fuckin' liberty, mate. I got my revenge at the duty free and stole loads of perfume. I showed them who the boss was. It was like Chinese whispers at the airport. Everybody seemed to know we had been arrested. Once home to Stansted, we caught a taxi home. We sighed with relief, then burst out laughing. What a holiday that was - no tan, no sea. Just a German police station.

Chapter 19 - Dad

I shall tell you a little story about how crafty my Dad was. He'd always have an angle to make a bit of cash, maybe that's where I get that side from. When I gave birth to my daughter Georgina, my mother-in-law Janet bought me a beautiful blue and white Mamas and Papas pram for the baby, which could also be converted to a pushchair. A few years later, my step-sister Kate moved back to stay at Dad's house. She was pregnant and really sick with it. She could not cope with living on her own so felt the need to stay with him. She was also single at the time with no one to support her.

One day, while I was having coffee with Dad he said, "I feel really bad you know. Kate's having the baby and I'd love to give 'er something for the baby. But I ain't got no money. She needs a pram."

"I'll tell ya what Dad, Georgie's outgrown 'ers it's a good'un, just needs a clean-up. Janet paid a fortune for it. She can 'ave it. I'll bring it round later in the week alright!"

And that was that. I took it round to Dad's house for Kate. A few months later, we - Kate and I - were engaged in conversation. She said, "Cheers for the pram Kim. I couldn't afford a brand new one. It's great, the price was just within my budget." I sensed something was seriously wrong here.

"'ang on a minute. What d'ya mean the price was just right?"

"The seventy five pounds, I gave it to yer Dad for you." I sighed with disbelief.

"The sneaky bastard. He said he wanted to give ya somefing for the baby so I gave it to 'im!"

That was Dad. He knew Kate was due a hundred pound grant from social security for the baby and he left her with twenty five pounds, two weeks supply of nappies, if she was lucky. Wanker! I can say this, but it still didn't stop me loving my Dad. I just accepted his faults. Kate felt the same. In the end, we couldn't help but laugh!

Like most people, I have experienced pain in my life. Mum died when she was fifty two years old. But the biggest heartbreak for me was losing Dad. He was my rock, my best friend and my hero. He raised three of my children and I guess I imagined he would be here forever. Learning to live without him at the time was my toughest challenge in life. He was so funny. Even when he was dying in hospital, he was still cracking jokes. As I said, he was my mentor and my hero. He still is.

I guess he was the only one in my life who could read me inside and out and left a huge void in my heart. I still love you, Dad. Even writing this is hard because the tears are welling up inside me. Pure emotion. He could be a cantankerous old bastard, no doubt about that. We were forever falling out, but that never ever changed the love I felt for him. That feeling will never leave me.

At the age of forty eight, he was diagnosed with kidney failure, a disease he had unfortunately inherited genetically from his father. It wasn't alcohol related whatsoever. Two of his sisters also had the disease. His father was treated in hospital by the famous Dr Roger Bannister, famed for running the first four minute mile in the film Chariots of Fire. The illness was a shock to Dad because he always led a very active life, then he found himself struggling with dialysis and he had to dramatically alter his lifestyle. He was very lucky in some respects. One summer, he received a transplant and it lasted for many years - just not forever and his body eventually rejected it.

Dave and I were on holiday in Spain, Menorca with the two girls Paris and Georgina. This is so vivid in my mind. It feels like yesterday when in fact he died in 2004. The holiday wasn't going as planned. The weather was crap. It was raining and we were all arguing. I tried to get a flight home but I couldn't. My gut instinct was telling me that something was amiss. I phoned Dad from Spain, "I'm waiting for you, Kim", he said. I thought why is he talking in riddles, is he drunk?

"What d'ya mean Dad?"

"Ah don't worry, just enjoy yer 'oliday." He was already in hospital but didn't want to spoil our holiday so said nothing.

I arrived home to shock and horror. Well, not a shock really, because he was in hospital. He had been in an out various times over the past few years. But I felt shock and horror due to the severity of his illness. One leg was completely infected and wasn't responding to treatment. To stop it spreading throughout his body, they needed to amputate the leg. The doctor then informed me that he was so weak, there was no guarantee that he would survive the operating table and if they left him with the infection, he would suffer extreme pain and probably survive for three months only.

There was also a third option - the hardest of all - to stop dialysing and let him die pain-free within forty eight hours in hospital, surrounded by his loved ones. I chose that option. With pain in my heart, I had the daunting task of informing my siblings the situation. I was filled with mixed emotions and a lot of resentment because most of them had never even bothered to visit him in years while he was alive and now they're allowed to cry by his bedside? But, I managed to put aside my personal feelings and notified them. He had a right to say goodbye to everyone. Then the circus began. Poor staff at St Helier's Hospital.

One-by-one, the siblings arrived with Maggie and her two sons, Dad's step sons. It was busy, busy, busy. My son Jimmy and I had reconciled a few years earlier and he grew to love his newly found Grandad. Damon, Ricky and Jade were there as were many of Dad's friends who wanted to say their goodbyes. I suppose I was so distraught by what was happening, it is all a little blurry about who was there and who stayed.

Maggie and Dad had separated but still kept in touch. He was the love of her life. The illness had made him unbearable to live with. He became bitter and it took its toll on their relationship. Eventually, she left him, but kept vigil with me, my other half Dave, Jimmy, and Ricky. We never left the hospital. My brothers Scott and Patrick were both present when the priest arrived to give him "the last rights". Scott couldn't bare it and he began to sob.

To see someone you love fade away before your very eyes is not something I would recommend. Kate was waiting for an emergency passport for her son because she had moved to Spain, but couldn't get there in time. Probably better for her because I don't think she could have handled seeing her stepdad like that. They were quite close. The family had a whip round to get enough money so my brother Lee could fly from Australia where he had lived for years.

Four days Dad hung in there, not forty eight hours for him, the stubborn old bastard. We were mentally and physically exhausted. Maggie joked, "If he carries on much longer, we're going to have to put a pillow on his head!" Emotions were high and a few heated family arguments broke out. Mainly my emotions burst out and at one point, security had to be called. Dad was comfortable, dosed up with morphine and occasionally murmured "leg of lamb and vodka."

He knew he was dying. How must that feel? It is hard to comprehend. At the end, Ricky and I were with him. He sighed then said, "Quick. Get out, Rick!" like he knew. Ricky refused to leave and I had the urge to run in his room. Then, just as I held his hand, and said "I love you and going to miss you," he took his laugh breath. He was finally at peace. It seems that my family only reunite at funerals which made me think, that's not right?

I took care of the funeral arrangements and, against everyone's wishes, partly due to the cost involved, I made sure he had a wicked send off. He had a glass horse drawn carriage. To cut costs, we agreed to walk from his house behind the carriage to Kingston Cemetery which was close by so didn't need the added expense of cars. It was December and a pretty cold morning when we began our walk towards the cemetery. People were standing in line and as we passed, they joined the procession.

I looked back to see a sea of people. There was half the estate and other friends walking with us. I never realised he was that popular. The police were on standby because they were looking for a small time criminal and convinced he may of shown his face. I arranged for a white dove to be set free and the wake was in "The Bull and Bush", the pub at the top of Dad's road - his local. He cannot say he didn't have a great send off because I made sure that he did.

Chapter 20 - Grief

I could not accept Dad's death. It was as simple as that. Everyone deals with grief in their own way. I spiralled out of control and chose to use alcohol and cocaine to numb my pain. I also began to smoke cigarettes heavily whereas before, I only smoked socially whenever at parties, for example. I lost track of everything, except for my love for shopping and the love for my daughter Paris. These two things were, in my eyes, the only reason I had the will to stay alive.

But Paris was witnessing her Mum hitting a self-destruct button because alcohol and drugs just heightened my existing emotions. Although I thought it was helping me, in fact it was doing the reverse and merely prolonged the process of healing from the pain. When I hurt, I push people away and that is exactly what I did to Dave. The more he tried to help me, the more I pushed him away and retreated into my shell. I became aggressive and we were constantly arguing and at each other's throats. Eventually, our relationship fell apart because of my behaviour and my incessant need for drugs and alcohol.

I got through about eight bottles of wine a week and at weekends I would binge on Jack

Daniels. Not to mention the amount of white powder I was snorting. Jesus, I am surprised I am still alive! I might as well had thrown my money down the drain and for what, to numb the pain? All I was doing was hurting myself and those who loved and cared for me. I knew I was making Dave's life miserable so I ended our relationship.

Months flew by and I carried on this lifestyle, until one day, I caught my reflection in the bathroom mirror and was pretty shocked at what I saw. Who was that person? Just before, Paris remarked that my belly looked as though I was pregnant. That comment must have stayed in my subconscious causing me to look at myself. My face was puffy with broken veins appearing, my stomach was bloated and even my arms became flabby. I looked like a different person. I decided there and then that I had to change and stop this behaviour. No more!

So I swapped one addiction for another. I joined a gymnasium and began eating properly. I also stopped taking drugs and drinking alcohol. I prepared myself healthy juices with fresh ingredients and slowly recuperated, not only physically, but mentally too. My healing process had begun. I quit the cigarettes again and said that I'll never again want to return to that dark place again. After a few months of my new healthy lifestyle, on occasions, I would have a few drinks with friends but this time, I was in control and the drug was not controlling me.

Chapter 21 - Funny memories

In my time, I've had a few close shaves and many funny stories. After a tough few chapters, I feel a bit of cheering up is needed all round!

Let me start with Maggie and Dad's wedding. Maggie had it in her head that, prior to their trip to the family court at the Strand, when obtaining my children's custody order, it would look far better to a judge that they were legally married. Although they lived together for years, they had never tied the knot and only then decided to do so. It was a pretty low-key affair – at the local registry office. Maggie was catering for herself and a few people back to the house after. Kate and I were the two witnesses. A few days before, I managed to get my hands on a stolen chequebook and card so I offered to get some food and alcohol for their wedding using it.

Now, Maggie was a very honest woman and not really criminal material but we agreed to meet. She drove me to Sainsbury's in Surbiton High Street. Her teenage son, Andrew, came too. He was about thirteen years old at the time.

Anyway, we had just finished shopping and proceeded to the till. I signed the cheque, the food was all bagged up and in the trolley when the young eagle-eyed boy on the till must have recognised the written name on the cheque book, which matched a name on their stolen list (in those days, the shops had written lists of recently stolen cheque books) and he called the supervisor. My instinct told me something was wrong so I told Maggie to take the food in the lift to the car park, load the car and fuck off very quick. She started running off like nervous Nerys. The supervisor was slow to materialise so I convinced the young boy I was just going to get a packet of cigarettes. Andrew was still there. I threw the hang bag with the evidence at Andrew and said, "Fucking run!"

I began to leg it as fast as I could up the high street. In the meantime, Andrew looked like he had robbed some old ladies handbag as he sprinted up the road clutching it under his arm. He said, when he stopped at the train station gasping his breath, that everyone was staring at him. I was still being chased by two young fit men dressed in brown Sainsbury's overalls. As much as I tried, I failed to out-run them and cut through the back of the train station and headed towards Nanny Bridget's house in Ewell Road. Maggie by this point had already sped home, driving like Cruella De Vil out of Sainsbury's multi-storey car park and arrived home, shaking, unpacking the shopping into her hallway and was relaying the episode to Dad.

"Don't leave the gear here. Get it out the 'ouse. They may come 'ere if they got yer number plate," Dad said. So they stashed the food elsewhere.

I made it into Nanny Bridget's house but the boys had seen me enter and were waiting outside. Andrew, bless him, had walked home with the bag. Well, he ran most of the way and Dad was ranting at him. The police surrounded Nanny Bridget's house and searched her house. They found me hiding in a suitcase in her attic so I was arrested.

Dad was distraught. "If she ain't released soon, the wedding tomorrow is off," he said.

Thankfully, I was released and the wedding went ahead, even though my Dad told the neighbours when they enquired about his smart suit, that he was going to a mate's wedding. Little Ricky was dressed as a Buckingham Palace homeguard that his brother Damon wore at my wedding. One of Dad's best friends arrived at the Registry Office with a carrier bag holding a bottle of Vodka. It was his wedding present for the happy couple.

Here's another fun story. Once in Woolworths, a friend and I filled two large bags with toiletries. I knew we were being followed by the store detectives. My friend wouldn't walk out of the shop but I did. Now, I was faced with the problem of getting to my car. It was a bright orange Opel Manta parked in The Bishop's car park. It was already loaded with stolen merchandise because we had been hitting the shops all day, going backwards and forwards to deposit our treasure in the car.

I legged it out of the shop and was being chased by two "undies" as I ran to my car. My friend, in the meantime, escaped on foot. I managed to get in and start the car before they arrived but, when I went to the ticket barrier, they both jumped on the car bonnet. That was their error. I saw red. I knew I had no time to insert my ticket so I put my foot to the floor and screeched out of the car park. I took the barrier with me and got away with that one. Nutty lady, I was in my late twenties and pretty crazy.

Another day in Kingston, there were a few of us in the car when the police pulled us over. They handcuffed my friend Gillian to the railings and, while they were doing that, I ran as fast as my little legs would carry me. I ran into Argos, found a box with a duvet inside, removed the duvet, got in then covered myself with the duvet. I remained perfectly still for about half an hour (good job no one wanted a new duvet), then I casually climbed out to receive some pretty strange looks by the other shoppers as I emerged from a quilt box. Being small has its advantages and I got away that day, the others were arrested.

I even engaged my brother Patrick to work for me. He owned a second hand car plot and business wasn't doing too well so he agreed to come shopping. We'd been shopping in Bentalls and had bags stuffed with the latest expensive trainers and tracksuits. But I needed to make a quick stop to Ravel's because Jade needed some new shoes. While we were there, Patrick put the bags down and some bastard stole them - ha ha ha – Karma! I was livid. I went mental and sacked him there and then. He then branched out on his own and, for some strange reason, he loved stealing prams and kept putting dolls inside them, acting as if they were actual babies. He must have been having a flashback from when I dressed him as a girl!

Even my brother Scott had a go at shopping with me. He joined the crew. He used to make me laugh which is unusual because I am usually deadly serious when shopping. Afterwards, Scott would delight in telling others that I forced him into the shops and that he did it against his free will.

"I don't wanna go. Nooo Kimmy, I pleaded with 'er," he'd say. "But she put 'er foot on me back and kicked me in the shops." Then he would roar with laughter and carry on with his story. "I tried to pull away but she just wasn't having any of it."

Then, he would change his voice into a crazy tone saying, "No Kimmy, the sales are on." Then we would both roar with laughter. He didn't like shopping with me. Scott used to say to me, "You've got a face like Crimewatch and a body like Baywatch," then he'd cackle with laughter.

Shopping with Scott, we had many close shaves. He will probably cringe when he reads this but one day, I wanted some pine furniture and already sussed out where to get it. I was distracting the shop assistant while Scott was loading the furniture into the car. All was going well until some nosey passerby realised what he was doing and ran into the shop to inform the assistant.

Scott drove off at top speed in one direction and I ran as fast as my little legs would take me in the other direction, only to run straight into the police and taken in for questioning. The police searched my house and took away all my pine furniture. They couldn't prove it was stolen and it wasn't from that shop, so they had to return it to me. The furniture we stole was never recovered because we had to sell it quickly. I guess Scott was right - the sales were on that day.

Ah Scott, I have so many memories of you, my brother. He was an avid golfer and had a friend who wanted a set of Ping golf clubs. Off we trotted to the sport shop in Surbiton - Scott, my friend Kelly and I. The plan was for Scott to keep the attendant occupied, engaged in conversation whilst Kelly and I stole the set of golf clubs. It worked a treat. In less than five minutes, we had the clubs and were out the door.

But the attendant knew something was up yet did not know that Scott was with us. Several times he tried to get away from Scott and move towards us, but he had him cornered and was saying things like "Excuse me, are you being rude? I am trying to ask for information as you don't appear remotely interested. I am a customer." I could tell by the man's body language he was suspicious and we got out. Scott joined us later and we laughed!

We didn't laugh as much as we did whilst trying to steal some fish. Yes, fish. I did say I had some strange requests from people. Anything new became a challenge to me. So, off Scott and I went to a Koi Carp place in Chessington. The fish were worth one thousand pounds each there! I grabbed a bag and a rod, just like that. I had seen the man in the shop doing so when he sold one but fuck he made it look so easy and that, it wasn't. For the love of God, I couldn't catch one. The little bastards kept getting away. Scott was in hysterics, "Come on Kim, give it some welly girl. They're getting away," He'd say pissing himself with laughter.

"Shut the fuck up, you try. It ain't as easy as it looks." I passed him the rod and he replied, "Okay, you little fuckers. Come to Daddy, come on," but he had as much success as me. "Fuck this," he said. "I know what, I'm gonna get me scuba diving gear on and a snorkel. That should bloody do it." We both cracked up laughing.

We didn't give up though. We were there a good half hour until we both called it a day and left crying with laughter. "You crank, why are we doing this?" he said.

"Just catch one of the little fuckers, they're worth shit loads of money." I said, sorry to say the fish won that day and I lost.

One of my better employees was Kelly. We worked well together until my brother Lee chose to seduce her. Actually, I think it was the other way round. I invited him round for a birthday meal and Kelly was there too. By the time dessert was served, Lee was having his own dessert in the form of oral sex performed by Kelly. He then had the cheek to order her to no longer shop with me and took her with him for a new life in Australia. He stole one of my best employees but it transpired that Kelly was not exactly in lerve with Lee. She ran off with his best mate. It happens all the time, you men and best mates - it's a myth.

Ooh, here's a funny story I nearly forgot to mention. I owned a pale blue German Fiat which resembled the three wheeled disabled cars that people used to drive - exact same colour too. It wasn't a sporty motor for me but I didn't care. The fact that it ran was all I cared about. Somebody sprayed canned white snow on it and wrote "NOB". I think it was one of the kids who did it. I never bothered to wash it off because it made me laugh whenever my daughter Georgina sat at the back, looking through the giant "O" with her bright red hair and everyone would stare.

Anyway, I parked the car outside WH Smith while I nipped quickly into Waitrose to get something for dinner with my teenage son Damon. My step-sister Kate waited in the car with her baby daughter Scarlett because she point blank refused to walk inside any shops with me. I made her a nervous wreck. I had tiger prawns and chicken up my coat sleeves. The security man followed me out of the store. He looked like John Cleese from Fawlty Towers, wearing a dark suit - tall and gangly. I told

Damon, "'Urry up, Damon. This arse 'ole's on me case."

The guard was closing in behind us as we made our way towards the parked car. I jumped into the driver's seat and Kate looked nervous because she knew something was amiss. "Quick Damon. Jump in the fuckin' car," I shouted.

The only problem we had was my car had two doors. Kate was sitting on the other seat with the baby so she couldn't dive in the back. By now, I was already revving the car. 'John Cleese' came alongside of me and he knew my name.

"Kim, if you don't come with me, I shall take your son instead," he said.

"Damon, get in the fuckin' car now," I demanded. With that, Damon dived through the open window on Kate's side and she hauled him in whilst I put my foot down and sped off with his legs hanging out.

Damn, I was parked in the wrong direction and faced a dead end of Kingston Market which meant I had no option but to turn the car around. I could still see 'Cleese' in the road. Fuck me, he was only standing right in my path trying to block me from driving past. So I put my foot to the floor, aimed right at him and just at the last minute, he jumped out of the way. I swerved.

"Fuck! You nutter," said Kate.

We laughed when we got home. I knew the police would arrive that night so, as I heard them pull up, I jumped into the loft - a common occurrence - or sometimes the neighbours garden. They didn't mind. Kate let them in and explained that I was not home. They were also looking for Damon who was in his room. They had a good look around but one, big burly policeman wouldn't enter his room because he had a phobia to spiders - and Damon had his pet tarantulas.

"Is that Damon?" the policeman asked Kate pointing at Damon.

"No, that's Ricky." she replied. I telephoned my solicitor Jerry and he made an appointment for us to resolve the misdemeanour at the police station together the following day.

I do miss that car I mentioned earlier. I had fond memories with it. Kate and I went out one night to Joe's wine bar in Richmond Bridge. It was a weeknight but it was her birthday so we went out anyway. I had stolen Kate a nice little black dress and, when I ripped the alarm off, there was a slight hole in the seam - but nothing noticeable. There were a group of young men, I think four of them, and one approached us.

"Alright girls, how's it going? Nice dress. Did you actually pay for that, or just rip off the alarm?" Fucking cheeky bastard. But he was spot on. We initially thought he was a member of the old bill, but later found out they were thieves from Hammersmith. We ended up joining their group and had a right laugh. They were really funny guys. When the bar closed, we went off with them to a bar in Kew then, somehow, Kate was in the other car with a guy called Mark and he took her to a party. Meanwhile, I was with the other guys in another car and they had a few chores to do. They never said as much, but we spent a few hours swapping cars. I think they were stealing cars. Later, I joined Kate at the party and we went home. We left my poor German Fiat in Richmond because the streets were busy and we were too embarrassed to be seen getting in it. Sadly, it got towed away and I never saw it again.

We went to Joe's wine bar a few times. That's where we met the actor that played Zammo from Grange Hill. Well, he was a sitting duck for us. We both had a few drinks so began to sing his famous anti-drug song, "Just say no," as loud as we could, which was pretty scary because, like Bridget the midget, I cannot sing. Neither can Kate. Zammo locked himself in the toilets and wouldn't come out until we stopped!

I have spent many times being chased by security. Eighty percent of the time, I always managed to escape because I always prepared for the worst and usually had an escape plan using my wits and initiative. On another occasion stealing from Bentalls, I knew that security saw me and my accomplice so I left the shop and tried to call her to abort mission, dump the merchandise and leave empty handed because I knew security were waiting for her. But when I tried to call her, she was engaged on another call. She ignored one of my strict rules of conduct so she left the shop with the goods and we both got arrested. She got the sack and I found myself on route to prison with a six month sentence. Silly mistakes like that lead to severe consequences - an example of someone that didn't listen to me. I had rules for a reason.

My son Jimmy had a rather strange request from one of his friends at college. Could I get him some Ann Summers vibrators? I thought about this one long and hard (sorry, a bit lame I know. I couldn't resist it), then once I located where they sold them, I stole ten. I thought that was the end of the subject but no. For fucks sake, they wanted more. I had another order for forty dildos which I fulfilled. I dreaded to ask why they wanted so many. I liked to think it made a lot of people very happy. That didn't stop Jimmy earning the nickname Dildo Jimmy.

Shopping with a friend, we stole a massive box of saucepans we both wanted. Again though, I saw we were being followed by the store detective so when we left the store, we ran and threw the box of saucepans into a parked van at the Market Place. We got away and later returned to retrieve our pans. It was a miracle they were still there and the van hadn't moved so we were chuffed. That night, we both dressed up and went out on the town, clubbing. Inside the club, there was a man I recognised but could not place his face. He approached me.

"Hello," he said.

"Do I know you?" I replied.

"Let me remind you. Today. Saucepans," he said.

"What you on about?"

Then it dawned on he was the man that had chased us through Kingston earlier that day.

"Prove it," I said, and we both laughed.

Another time, I spent the day in Wimbledon stealing from the shops and my car was rammed with stolen goods. I had Sylvia, my son Ricky and his former girlfriend Sally in the car and my seat belt was tucked under my arm and not over as it should have been. The police stopped our car. There were a lot of heavy heartbeats going on in the car.

"What's up mate?" I said.

"Madam your seat belt should be worn over your shoulder and not like that,"

"Ah I'm sorry. I just find it uncomfortable like that," I said.

"Well, if you go to Kwik Fit, you can buy some soft seat belt covers designed to make it more comfortable. I'm not gonna fine you today but make sure you put in over yer shoulder from now on, then go and buy those cover thingys, alright!"

"Fank you, officer," I said while driving off. Thank fuck he didn't want to look in the car. I had thousands of pounds worth of stolen goods all with the tickets still on. Phew!

One night, as I danced the night away, I entered into a competition to win a free holiday for two. The winner had to come up with the most erotic fantasy. I obviously made up some load of crap fiction involving a teenage boy and confessing after to a randy priest. I won. But, before they awarded me my prize, I then had to relay the sound of an orgasm over the microphone like in When Harry Met Sally. No problem. I had obviously faked loads in my first relationship and experienced quite a few.

I was so chuffed I won the holiday, I took my friend Justin, a lodger of mine, with me. Yay, we won a holiday to Kavos in Greece. We were dancing the night away in a Greek nightclub when the local mafia boss took a shine to us. Fuck that, we made a hasty retreat drinking with the mafia in a foreign country. I wouldn't even do it in England.

In my twenties, I thought maybe I could make a bit of money doing a bit of modelling. Not catwalk stuff. I knew that was way beyond my league, but glamour modelling. So I joined an agency in London. It was called Star Now Model Agency and had a pretty small office in the centre of the capital. Nothing really came of it except a few photoshoots with me and a few other girls. We did some shots in sexy underwear followed by another shoot at Epsom Racecourse. I remember one of the girls had a few stretch marks so they positioned me in front of her to cover them. It was supposed to be for a calendar but none of us saw any money from it. I was told that these agencies were charlatans and had probably sold the pictures to Japan where we were never likely to find out about it.

Another night, I was in The Cap In Hand Pub when a model scout was looking for talent. The pub was rammed with people. He took me under the light and checked out my face. I was probably in my late twenties. He said, "Shame about your complexion." Bloody cheek, fucking liberty. Well, that was the end of my modelling days.

Another time I was dancing the night away in a club in Kingston, a Madonna song came on and the DJ encouraged me to get up on the stage where he was. I was a bit tipsy and I stripped right down to my G-string and six inch high heels. Everyone was clapping until a young man stripped down to his boxers and jumped up on the stage with me.

"Wow, you are one sexy lady," he said.

The next thing I knew, his girlfriend marched over and gave him the biggest slap ever. He nearly fell off the stage. It served him right. I ran with my clothes to the toilets to get dressed and twisted my ankle in the process.

I always used to attract the men because I was pretty outgoing and funny. Many girls used to be jealous. I suppose if I wasn't attractive, they wouldn't have minded. I like to have banter with the opposite sex. It's all a bit of fun. It didn't mean I wanted to run off with them. I guess I prefer the company of men and they appreciated my sense of humour more than up tight girly girls. Men would always want to buy me drinks but I preferred to buy my own. That way, you don't get stuck with some boring bastard obliged to stay in his company just because he bought you a drink. One night a man asked me to dance and I said "No, yer alright mate." I tried to put him off. "You wouldn't wanna dance wiv me if yer knew what I did for a living."

"Try me," he said.

"Okay, I'm a professional shoplifter," I said. He laughed and didn't believe me and insisted on the dance so I obliged.

"I shall tell you what I do but not til after we dance," he said. "Or else you won't dance with me." We danced until the music stopped. He said, "I'm C.I.D and work for Scotland Yard." He wasn't joking. Oh, how I laughed with my mates later. It was fucking funny.

When I lived in my house in Teddington, I briefly dated a local young man from Kingston. His occupation was robbing garden centres and bathroom showrooms in the early hours of the morning. My house in Teddington was located within walking distance to a pine store warehouse. One morning I woke up, jumped out of bed, pulled the curtains and fuck me, my normally bare garden was full of pine garden furniture. Even a fucking bird table. He hadn't even warned me that he was going to store his loot there. Bloody check - what a fuckin' liberty. What if the old bill had spun my house? Anyway, that was a very brief relationship.

If I say something to someone about anything, I genuinely mean what I say. I find it hard to understand that others say things they don't really mean. One evening, I had been drinking in Dad's local and one of his friends George offered to take me, my son Ricky and a few others to Kingston for a Chinese meal so off we all went. The food was lovely and afterwards George invited us back to his house for more drinks. Whilst we were there, he explained that the following day he was going on holiday but while he was gone, I could look after and have full use of his car. Nice one, I thought. It was a luxury BMW worth about forty thousand pounds.

Anyway George fell asleep and I drove the car home. I forgot to turn on the back lights and soon the flashing blue lights of nick nick, as Jim Davidson would say, were in my mirror, so I pulled over.

"Excuse me madam, you have not turned on the back lights," said the officer.

"Oh sorry about that, I'll do it now," I replied.

"Actually, can you do me a favour and blow into this bag please."

Shit, fuck. I knew I was over the limit. I blew in the bag and got arrested for drink driving. The car was impounded at Kingston police station. The following morning, George woke and was searching for his car. He rang Mick the landlord from the local pub, who rang Dad, who then rang me.

"I ain't got 'is car. The police 'ave it!" I explained to Dad what had happened.

"Kim, 'e's going on 'oliday today and he's got his cash in that car, two thousand five 'undred notes, and 'is suitcase in the boot!"

"Well 'e shouldn't 'ave told me I could 'ave the car." Simple as that. You cannot tell me I can take something because I take people at their word, just as I am. We chuckled about it later and I am not sure if he actually made his flight the poor man.

In my late twenties, I had another fling with a young man and one night I decided to surprise him. So, after my shower, I dressed in sexy red underwear, fresh makeup, nice earrings, fresh perfume and super high heels then put on a full length cream fur coat over the top. I then called a cab and arrived at his house unannounced about ten o'clock at night. He let me in and when I took my coat off, well you can imagine the rest. Steamy passionate sex. He enjoyed it so much that the ritual carried on for a further eighteen months. I just changed the sexy outfits and bought many from the Ann Summers catalogue. It was good fun and a bit of a thrill for me, pretending to be a high class call girl, but without any payment. It was pure sex.

There was no emotion involved and the next morning, I would have to do the walk of shame homeward bound in a taxi half naked, wearing the coat of shame.

Chapter 22 - Patrick

From a young age, my brother Patrick was on a rocky road as a used car salesman. Despite this, he was very driven and when he reached middle aged, he was pretty much sorted in life. He had expensive cars, including a Bentley, a huge house, and designer clothes. He also married his long-term girlfriend Anna in St Lucia. They were together for years and produced two beautiful children, Charlotte and Patrick Jnr. I hadn't seen Patrick for a long time, to be truthful, since Mum died. It seemed my siblings only sought me out when they were in trouble or at a crossroads in their lives. I assumed, because I hadn't seen Patrick for a while, that he was happy in his life and everything was hunky dory. At that time, he and Anna separated and he had a new life and new girlfriend.

I was at home in Teddington when I received a phone call from my son Ricky.

"Mum, it's Uncle Patrick. He's in a coma in Guildford Hospital. Everyone's there. You gotta get yerself up there, 'e's got a tumour on 'is brain and they don't think 'e's gonna last much longer."

I slumped onto the sofa. Words were failing me. I didn't know how to respond. My baby brother dying. He was only forty seven. This wasn't happening.

"Mum, Mum are ya there?"

"Yes Rick. Okay," I said putting the phone down. I sat in silence trying to comprehend Ricky's words. A brain tumour? No, they must have got it wrong. Patrick was sorted. He had all that a man could want and now he gets a brain tumour?

I didn't want to go to the hospital. I remembered how painful it was to see Mum and Dad as they were about to take their last breaths. I wanted my memory of Patrick to be as I remembered him - healthy and laughing - as he always was. He was like the jolly policeman. Ricky kept me informed on what was happening. Apparently his head was badly swollen and it was only a matter of time until he died. There was nothing that the doctors could do to save him. The phone rang again. It was Ricky.

"Mum, they are all waiting for ya at the hospital." I had made up my mind and I was not going.

"I know Rick, I aint goin'. I wanna remember him how he was, not with a swollen head and about to die. I'm sorry but it's my choice. Please don't ask me again, bye."

The thought of seeing Patrick there, weak and dying, just stirred up other feelings about Mum and Dad and I could not see him like that. I felt the need to stay strong for everyone and didn't think I would be able to if I saw him like that.

I didn't have much involvement in the funeral arrangements. None of us did. It was left to the new girlfriend and his new in-laws. He had a huge house and expensive cars and looked after her and her family financially so I was sure that they would ensure that he had a splendid send off with no expense spared. All I had to do was arrange for some flowers for him. I chose a pink and white bouquet in the form of a crash helmet because in his youth he was mad about motorbikes. As a young teenager, he had a scrambler bike and wore the leather suit and a crash helmet.

I didn't have a lot of contact with my family about Patrick until the day of the funeral when we all made our way to a church in Claygate. It is all a bit of a blur. Several people got up and said a few words about Patrick. I remember my brother Robbie was one of them. A few of the others had words prepared but were too upset to read them out. I was sitting next to Charlotte. She was sobbing her little heart out so as I sat down, did a little dance and said to her, "Yer Dad is now dancing up and down this church." She smiled and managed a slight laugh. I always try and deflect sadness with a little humour, but deep inside my heart was heavy with sadness too. We were all affected, probably because he was so young and it was such a shock.

There really was a mixed crowd there - the family, Anna and her family, the new "family" and his stockbroker friends. After the ceremony, we all went outside to look at the flowers and there was a photo of Patrick. I had to look twice. The photo was not a very flattering one. I didn't recognise him. He looked awful and bloated. He was always a handsome man.

"That ain't my bruvver," I said out loud.

"Yes that's my Patrick. He did love his food," said a woman to the left of me.

"And you are?"

"I'm Patrick's mother-in-law. Are you Kim?"

"Yeah," I replied.

"Oh, I've heard lots about you," she said.

"All bad I hope, and it's all true."

I walked away. I did not like the woman. I took an instant dislike to her. My sixth sense told me she was not a nice person. Then I met her daughter, Melanie - it was clearly the case of like mother like daughter. I didn't take to her either. Patrick and Melanie, at that time, recently had a child together. Considering she had just lost, supposedly, the love of her life, she did not shed one tear and was walking around with the baby and Patrick's best friend. They looked a little too cosy for my liking and I was not the only one that thought that. She was a lot younger than Patrick and a big girl, not his usual type - a bit chubby.

Off we all went to the wake where I anticipated a good spread to celebrate his life, especially because I had been told we were going to his local. We must have been there about forty minutes buying drinks and reminiscing when I suddenly said, "Where's the food, I'm hungry?" Well, on my life they brought out some crisps and nuts. I was livid. That was it. Fucking crisps and nuts for my wealthy brother who supported not only Melanie, but her parents too?

To top it all off, Melanie refused to let Patrick Jnr and Charlotte have anything that belonged to their father. She was so disrespectful. Not even an old shirt each, or a book, nothing. The new family portrayed themselves as greedy blood suckers and I wondered what Patrick saw in them. I didn't think he was that much of a fool. I'd like to think of him when he was young and happy - with Anna and the children - not the new vampire blood sucking family.

When we returned to Kingston, me and my siblings arranged our own wake for Patrick. We made sure it went with a bang. We had great food, a banquet fit for a king, singing and dancing, a Karaoke machine. We let off some fireworks and, most important of all, had all his family and close friends together. No vampires allowed.

Chapter 23 - Lee

I've already mentioned that whilst growing up, I had a particular soft spot for my brother Lee. He suffered from stomach troubles but the doctors seemed to ignore his pleas for help and he spent his entire childhood suffering. He only got it sorted out when he became an adult. Lee was my "lil shit legs", a term of endearment I used for him. He had a beautiful smile, huge brown eyes and a nasty temper when he lost it, which wasn't often. He lived in Australia for many years but we spoke regularly on the telephone. On one phone call, he said that he missed his family and was coming to England to visit us all. I was elated and couldn't wait to see him. He had a great sense of humour and always made me laugh. Well, not just me. He made everyone laugh.

When Lee was in England, one Thursday morning, I was doing housework when he rang. At that point, he was staying at our sister Tracy's house.

"Kim, it's me. Can I come and stay at yours? I've had enough of it 'ere. She's doing my head in. I've gotta get out of 'ere."

I could tell by his tone of voice that he was annoyed. I wasn't sure what had been said between them but he was in a rage.

"Calm yerself down. Yea no problem, get a cab 'ere."

So within the hour, Lee arrived in a taxi with his luggage. We hugged, cracked a few jokes and then I made him a delicious lunch at Kimmy's café. I am well known for feeding my guests like a Jewish mother.

"So, what's the matter wiv you and Trace?"

"Ah, she wants to throw a huge party for me and I don't wannit. I haven't been feeling well, so I said no and now she's ranting, saying I'm rude and an ungrateful shit. She just wants an excuse to have a party. It ain't for me, it's for 'er!"

"Ah, never mind. You can stay 'ere." So we chatted for hours and then we both had an early night.

The following morning I came downstairs and Lee looked dreadful. "Are ye alright mate? You don't look well!" He just looked at me but didn't reply.

"Okay, that's it. Get yer coat I'm taking ya to West Middlesex 'ospital. No arguing, yer coming."

He didn't want to go, but he had no choice. I wasn't taking any chances because he looked dreadful. Something was wrong. Once at the hospital, they carried out various tests and kept him in for a few days until the results were all back and he received the devastating news. Like Dad, he had kidney failure. After all he had been through as a sickly child, now this. Life didn't seem fair.

When they finally discharged him from hospital, he came back to stay with me and I looked after him, cooked him nutritional meals and made sure he was cared for in every manner possible. We talked and talked when the subject about dying arose. I didn't quite know how, but anyway it did.

Lee said, "Kim, I'm scared about dying."

"Shut up, yer not goin' nowhere mate. Me? I'll probably drop dead stealing in a shop, trying to rip an alarm off," we laughed.

It was soon time for his holiday visit to end and he was returning home in Australia. Jimmy, Paris and I took him to the airport and when he finally went through to catch his plane, we were all in floods of tears. It was very emotional. Worse because I knew he was ill and that he had no family in Australia.

I didn't hear from him for about a week and then he finally called to say that he was home safely and adopted a new puppy naming it "Little Kidney". We cracked up about that. It was a very cute little puppy and Lee adored him. The next time Lee telephoned was from his hospital bed in Australia.

"Hi Kim, I'm in 'ospital at the moment and they're not as good as England. If I wanna transplant I think I've got more chance in England," he said.

"Lee, I was finking the same. At least 'ere, you've got yer family. I'm gonna speak to the others and we will get ya 'ome." So I spoke to all my brothers and sisters. We all had a whip round and collected enough money to pay for his flight home to England.

Once in England, I didn't really see much of Lee. He was staying with Sylvia and at Tammy's house. He also had a close female friend that he stayed with from time-to-time. She was only a friend but they seemed to have a lot of love for each other. He rang me occasionally, then the phone calls got fewer and fewer. I didn't mind. I knew he was around the family and being looked after and I was happy enough doing my own thing.

Then one day I received a text. Lee wrote, "Kim, I need your help. I have no money and nowhere to live. I need to stay at yours." I found this extremely rude because he hadn't bothered to ring me in ages and there was no please. He just assumed that he was coming to stay with me and telling me! I didn't really mind him staying but he smoked weed - a lot of weed. I couldn't bear the smell nor did I want that sort of thing around my daughter Paris. I said no to him and he didn't message me again about it. He was obviously pissed off. Plenty of my sisters and brothers smoked weed, why couldn't he stay with them?

I found out later that he was staying with Tammy and eventually he got his own small place. Now Tammy was his super sister and they became really close. He had to dialyse three times a week at St Helier's hospital, just as his own Dad had done years ago. On his way home, he usually popped into Tammy's place because she cooked him dinner.

Then one Friday, everyone was phoning around frantically looking for Lee. He hadn't arrived at Tammy's house for his dinner. Nobody had seen him, not even the hospital. Why hadn't the hospital checked his flat when they went to collect him for his dialysis treatment? Were they not worried when they had no answer? Without the treatment, he would die. Surely they should have notified someone?

By Monday, Tammy was worried sick and went round to his flat banging on the door. Again as had happened previously there was no answer. Tammy is a very tiny lady and she managed to climb thorough a small window into the flat. The kitchen tap was running and she found Lee curled up on the floor by the door. She tried to wake him but it was no good. He was dead. I cannot even begin to think what that must have been like for Tammy! Sheer pain. It must haunt her sometimes. To this day, I doubt if she can ever truly recover from that ordeal. He must have been lying there all alone, all weekend. That breaks my heart.

Once again we faced another family reunion for yet another funeral. Tammy and Tracy arranged the funeral. None of us had a lot of money but we agreed to chip in eighty pounds each. Tammy collected the money and I paid mine to her straight away. I heard she had to wait a while to collect money from the others.

Tracy arranged for the flowers. They were meant to resemble a packet of reefers (cigarette papers) because he enjoyed smoking weed. But it didn't resemble anything. I kind of knew that Tracy would mess up the flowers so I had ordered my own in the shape of a guitar with blue and white flowers. Mine looked good and put the others to shame. I also paid one hundred and twenty pounds for a photo of Lee blown up and put onto canvas to go on top of his coffin.

I didn't want to go to the funeral and got myself into a real state because of it. Scott was shocked because he'd never seen me like that. I wore jeans and a blue jumper because I knew in my heart that Lee would not want me to wear black. I was sobbing and could not stop. "I don't want to go," I said in between sobs. I was never this bad at any of the other funerals. It was only a couple of years ago that I had said goodbye to Patrick and now Lee, "my lil shit legs."

The pain was unbearable and I couldn't cope. "Stop the car, pull over," I urged Scott. As the car pulled over, I opened the door and vomited everywhere. I had to go for Lee's sake and I had his picture with me for the coffin, which was important to me. Arriving at the ceremony was a bit of a blur because I had sobbed my way to the church. Once seated and the service began, I looked around and I started to panic. Where was my picture?

I began to get frantic. Where was my picture and why was it not on the coffin? I began to scream out loud, "Where's my picture?" I looked at Tracy. Again I screamed, "Where's my picture?" By this stage I was screaming like a nutter and all eyes were on me. Tracy replied, "Be quiet Kim, it's outside."

Well, I saw red like a raging bull. "You fuckin' what? Get 'is picture NOW! Now! How dare you. I want 'is picture now." I was screaming hysterically. Tracy knew I wanted the picture for the coffin. How dare she leave it outside. Sylvia's daughter Julia jumped up and went outside to get the picture. By this time, I was out there too. I was going ballistic, shouting and screaming. Julia took me by the arm.

"C'mon Kim. You need to say goodbye. Let's go back inside," said Julia.

So I went back inside. I was still upset. I felt his send-off had no style and not what he deserved. If I was allowed to change one day in the future, I'd hold another service in Lee's honour. With a bit of style. What he deserved.

Afterwards, everyone cracked jokes about my "nut out" and that Lee would be laughing because it wasn't a family get together if I didn't kick off over something. The wake was held at Sylvia's house, but I wasn't in the mood to be around certain individuals so I went home. They kept calling me to come round so eventually I did return. I got completely trashed on alcohol and began abusing everyone, in a good way. I had my funny head on or so I was told. I don't remember much. It's still a bit hazy. There is not one day that I do not think about my family, especially the ones I have lost. Writing about them all here had been extremely difficult, but also therapeutic.

Chapter 24 - Happy Christmas

One year, I invited my brothers Scott and Michael to spend Christmas with me. I hadn't seen them in years but we had all recently reunited at Lee's funeral. It's mad that our clan only seemed to get together for funerals but this is the reality of The Farrys. Every family funeral, I would think inside "Why are we all here?" We didn't spend time with them when they were alive so now we are all here crying for them. It was pure hypocrisy. I would look around me, see all those crying and think, fake tears. It's all bollocks. We didn't even like each other. Not all of us but many of the family members clashed.

Anyway, I found out that Scott and Michael had not celebrated Christmas since Mum had died. I was horrified and insisted that they both spent the festive season with me and some of my children. Why didn't they ring me and come for Christmas? My house is always open to all especially at Christmas time. Then again, I hadn't rung any of them, so it worked both ways. Maybe we should have stayed in touch a lot more.

Well, it turned out to be one of the best Christmases I ever had. Everything seemed perfect that year - the presents, the food and most of all, the company. We all got on like a house on fire, telling the kids funny stories from our childhood. With Scott around, it was always a laugh every minute because he takes after Dad and is incredibly funny. They loved my cooking, especially my roast potatoes. Scott joked, "That's how it should be. Loads of roasties. Not like Sylvia's dinners - she only serves three per person."

We laughed nonstop and ate like Kings. Lobster and prawns as a starter, followed by turkey and beef, then pudding was old fashioned trifle. Cheese and biscuits, grapes were later washed down with umpteenth bottles of champers. Oh yes, Christmas at my house always used to mean the best. Laugh? We were roaring that day. Mostly over how cranky I could be at times! Thinking about it, boys. We need to repeat that!

Chapter 25 - Jay

Love is a strange thing and I believe I experienced love four times until I met my current boyfriend, Jay. The love I feel for Jay is much more intense than anything I have ever felt before. We are way past the honeymoon stage. We have been together for five years now and hopefully for many more to follow.

We met purely by chance. It was an unfortunate event in my daughter Georgina's life that brought us together. My daughter was attacked one night as she left a nightclub by three Canadian girls. Georgie took off her high heel shoe to defend herself and battered one of her assailants but the judge chose to make an example of her and she was sentenced to three and a half years in prison. It angers me when I think of all the lenient sentences passed out to sex offenders but I shall refrain from ranting about that subject and stick to my story. Georgie asked me to contact Jay and arrange for his brother to visit her in prison because they were very close friends. I had been single since Dave and I separated seven years previous, and you know that saying - once you have been in prison for eight years you become institutionalised.

Well, maybe that applies to single people too, so thank fuck I met Jay.

Jay was far from the normal type of man I go for, but we had an instant connection. I had seen him around in Kingston and at Georgie's court hearing. He is a very caring warm individual, not only with me but also with my daughter Paris too. That is very important to me because, for once in my life, it is not just about me. Paris and I are a package. We come together, and whoever loves me, needs to love my family too.

What can I say about Jay? He is an amazing person in my life and we have helped each other so much. I cannot begin to describe how happy he has made me. I have never felt this way about any of my other relationships and sincerely mean that. He has taught me how to love in another dimension - real love. We have been through a hell of a lot together. Amazingly enough, we managed to come out far stronger. The bond we share is unreal.

Our relationship has proved the cynics and sceptics wrong. Even my own children disapproved at first. Despite our age difference, we are making our relationship work and are good together. Apparently I am a cougar and cradle snatcher because he is thirty years younger than me. It is fine for Joan Collins and other famous Hollywood stars, but not for me? People judged us and, to be honest, I am pretty happy with that. I do not give a flying fuck what anyone else thinks. I never have and I never will!

I look young for my age, or so I have been told. Shit they are not lying, are they? I keep in shape. I work hard to look and feel good for myself. What matters to Jay and I is that we truly care about each other and make each other happy. Some people even had the audacity to make venomous remarks about us but hey, that is clearly their problem and not ours.

Maybe we will get married in the future. Who knows what the future holds? Only this time, second time round, I will definitely be smiling. I am one lucky lady to have met such a perfect match. He is my best friend, my knight in shining armour. We are soulmates. Jay, your parents should be very proud to have raised such a caring gentleman.

Chapter 26 - Living Nightmare

I love to be surrounded by beauty. An Englishman's home is his castle, or in my case, an Englishwoman's home is her castle. I was pretty settled in my beautiful three bedroom house in Teddington, on a small housing estate. I lived there for twenty six years and, throughout those years, constantly updated it and had totally reformed it. I had expensive furnishings - bought and stolen - and made it my home. Living there was the longest I had ever stayed in my life.

This house was very dear to my heart. Not only had I made it cosy and a proper home, but it also held very precious memories to me. My Dad coming over for his Sunday dinner, many children and family gatherings, many Christmas and New Years were spent happily in this house. I would probably still be living there now if it wasn't for this one particular Saturday night - the night of horror, when my entire life was turned upside down in the space of hours.

I had given up the alcohol and drugs after the dark place I saw myself in during my grief for Dad but when I met Jay, I occasionally joined in a mad party night because, being young, he liked to party. It wasn't much - just every now and then. That night, my daughter

Paris was away on holiday with her friend for a week, so Jay came to the house for drinks and we had a little cocaine. All was going well, until he said he wanted to leave. I got a little stroppy because I didn't want him to go, and we had a silly little row before he left. I was a bit pissed off with him for going and I carried on drinking alone.

A few weeks earlier, some of Georgina's friends knocked on the door and Paris answered because I was in the kitchen cooking the dinner. "Mum it´s some of Georgie's friends", she shouted.

"What d'they want, I'm busy. 'ang on?" I then went to the front door. When I arrived, one of them began to speak. "We just need Georgie's prison numba cos we wanna go an see 'er."

I looked at him then said, "Alright, giv me yer numba an I'll text it to ya. I'm busy right now." So he did and that was that. Later, I texted him her prison number and thought nothing more about these boys. I did however receive a flirty reply from the boy which I ignored completely.

Getting back to that Saturday, Jay had left and I decided to take a nice bath. When I finished, my phone rang. Because I was hoping Jay would call, I answered the phone. But it was not Jay but these friends of Georgie's. I was high on alcohol and drugs when I answered the phone.

"We're in the area and wondered if we could pop round for a drink?"

"No problem, pop over," I replied.

I thought why fucking not? It was Saturday party night. The more the merrier! I tried to ring Jay to tell him to come back because people were coming over for drinks but there was no reply. I assumed he fell asleep. So I got dressed and awaited their arrival. Soon enough three of them arrived at my door.

One left to go to the shop and buy some alcohol so I invited the other two into my home. They seemed pleasant enough and I was pretty off my face. I knew I already had enough to drink so decided that I would not drink anymore alcohol. We sat in my front room and the other guy soon returned from the shop with brandy and a bottle of something else alcoholic that was green. They proceeded to pour me a glass of the green stuff but I didn't really like the taste and kept saying so. But they insisted, "No, drink it. It's really nice."

Out of the corner of my eye, I noticed that my Blackberry phone, next to the fish tank, had disappeared, and so had the boy wearing the hat. Where had he gone, back to the shop again? I was waiting for a telephone call from Paris and started to sense something was wrong and began to get a bit frantic. "Where's my fuckin' phone? It's gone? I need my fuckin' phone."

One of the guys began to speak. "It's okay. Relax. 'e's just borrowed it to call 'is mum while 'e's at the shop. 'e be back in a minute." Then they distracted me from the phone. "Cheeky fucker, I need my phone," I replied. I don't really remember much at that point except I began to feel really strange and sat on the sofa, dizzy and faint.

My next recollection was when I awoke in my bed. To this day, I have no idea how I got from my sofa upstairs to my bed. My top clothing remained but my bottoms and underwear had been removed. Next to me in the bed was one of the guys, Gerard Collins. I tried to leap out of bed but my legs felt strange. They felt paralysed and I trembled, feelings I had never experienced in my life. It wasn't pleasant. I did not like feeling like this.

"What the fuck is going on?" I screamed.

"You wanted sex, you wanted it," he kept repeating.

"No fuckin' way mate. Where's my phone?"

I looked around my bedroom. It had been ransacked. All my things clothes, everything, were strewn across the floor - even underwear and my vibrator they had thrown into my daughter´s bedroom. The boy upstairs was trying to calm me down and I managed to make it downstairs. All I wanted was my phone but my brain couldn't focus properly. For the first time in my life I felt utterly helpless and scared. These three young men I had invited into my home violated me and trashed my beautiful home.

Paris had a small dog that Dave and I bought her and they were throwing the poor dog backwards and forwards playing catch with her for their amusement. I could see the dog was distressed and tried to stop them but felt powerless. I could not grasp the concept of why I felt this way. "Please, please," I pleaded. "Leave the dog alone!" They then took the dog into the kitchen and Luke said with a chilling voice, "If ya don't let me take you upstairs and fuck ya, this dog is going in the microwave, ha ha ha."

I tried to attack him but my body was not working properly. It was all out of sync and I couldn't defend myself. Glasses and cups went flying everywhere. I managed to rip off one of their t-shirts from his back. I tried the house phone but it was not working and thought I had been cut off. My mind and body were not in coordination. I had been drugged but did not realise it. Then they put the dog in the microwave.

235

"Okay, okay. I'll do it," I screamed. "Please let the dog go!" I then went upstairs with Luke. He pushed me onto the bed. "I really don't want ya to do this," I said, but my words were useless. He was not listening to me. He ignored me and began to rape me.

During the ordeal, Luke hit his head on the shelf above my bed. I felt physically sick but he wasn't here for long. Then I heard a loud bang and he jumped up and ran downstairs. As I lifted myself from the bed, the youngest of the three was standing there. He came forward. "Are you OK?" he said. What sort of a fucking question was that? Of course I wasn't okay! I had just been raped by his two friends!

"NO. NOW FUCK OFF OUT MY 'OUSE," I screamed. They all left.

I went downstairs and found the dog shaking, trembling all over, sitting in the kitchen. I scooped her in my arms and ran to lock the front door. They had stolen money, two phones, some of my jewellery and trashed my home. I tried the house phone once more but nothing. It was still dead. I soon realised it was merely unplugged, so I plugged it back in and sat on the sofa. I began to sob. At first, it was a sniffle, then an uncontrollable wave of immense despair came over me. My entire body was sobbing, the tears would not stop flowing.

I must have sat, weeping for about half an hour sobbing, rocking myself. I then cleaned my face and called the police.

"999, what's your emergency?" At first, I couldn't speak but then managed to say, "I've been raped and robbed."

I then took the dog upstairs and crawled into my daughter's bed with the dog and fell asleep. The police arrived and took a DNA swab from me for a medical. It was all very degrading but I knew I needed to do this if there was any chance of convicting them for what they did to me. Doing it may prevent them from doing it to other girls in the future.

Chapter 27 - Why?

I could not get my head round why, or even how, it had happened. It happened so fast. I felt totally violated and humiliated and that, worse of all, I let my children down just at the point when our relationships were improving. I retreated into my shell like a tortoise, not wanting to face anything. How does anyone recover from something like that? I really did not have any answers.

I later found out that these boys had done this before. There were other victims. I also heard they would brag about their actions. The police tried to arrest them but they went into hiding for eight months until they were finally caught. They were remanded in prison until the trial began. It was a complete farce, considering the delicate nature of the charges. This was a rape case, yet the first jury were allowed to go on holiday so a retrial was declared for nine months later. I'd waited long enough and then they declared a retrial because the jury were on fucking holiday?

Another nine months of anguish followed - what sort of a justice system was that? The first judge was a lady who specialised in rape and even she was pretty outraged that it was declared a retrial. It is no wonder that rape victims sometimes fail to report the crimes. To relive the experience in a courtroom of people was horrific for me, let alone other victims. I felt like I had to prove my innocence yet I was not the one on trial. I was like Jodie Foster in The Accused.

How the fuck is a jury allowed to take a holiday? This meant I had to testify twice. Once was traumatic enough. Sometimes, we live in a sick world. I testified behind a screen because I never wanted to see their faces again. I purposely banned any family members there because I did not want them to hear the sordid details, but a friend came with me. She overheard the accused families saying, "Why the fuck would they want to rape 'er? She's ugly?" What a disgusting thing to say!

At the second trial the verdict came back as 'Not Guilty'. Even the police's jaws were on the floor. They had all the forensic evidence, had even found traces of the drug in my glass. It all pointed to a guilty verdict yet the judge declared them innocent. They were so cocky, all laughing amongst them and threatened to "finish me off." I sobbed again at the result. How could they be allowed to roam the streets and I was not their only victim.

Justice? Fuck off!

The police requested for a retrial but I wanted it all to end and said no more. I couldn't take it anymore. There were some vile rumours being spread throughout the Kingston community that I was lying and wanted them to do it. If that was the case, then why on earth would I report it to the police and drug myself? The guys were also terrorising my children. They were receiving threats. They even offered me money at one stage to drop the charges. Even so-called family members were saying, "Oh, they wouldn't do that. They're nice boys." Yes, you Lauretta. Invite them round one night for drinks. Go on, I dare you!

They forced me out of my beautiful home. There was no way I could live there ever again, not after that. They not only violated my body, but something inside me died too. Mentally, I was not the same person as before.

Chapter 28 - The Aftermath

I had to move away because I could no longer bear to set foot in my own home. While I made my roots and lived happily for twenty six years there, all it held now were sick and traumatic memories.

In my current home, I have a rape alarm fitted. Before then, I stayed between friends and relatives. From building up my health and strength, I rapidly deteriorated into a skinny, sunken human being. My physical and mental states were both affected by my ordeal. I aged overnight and looked about ninety.

I am not completely sure how many months passed by because, like before when I was in pain, I pushed people away and turned to drugs and alcohol. Numbing away the pain seemed the best way to spend the days. Christmas passed and I was staying with my son Ricky and his girlfriend. And, as all families do, we had a huge bust up and all fell out. It was then and there I decided enough was enough. Time for me to go home and face my demons. We were all getting on each other's nerves. I had out stayed my welcome and us falling out gave me the kick up the arse that I needed to return home and try and move on with my life.

My son Jimmy drove me to the house and my heart was beating with anxiety. I entered the house slowly and with caution. It was exactly the same state that I had left it on that fateful night. The house felt cold and haunted, not my cosy home I spent years creating. I fought back my tears. Those bastards were not going to get the better of me.

Throughout my life, my eyes have always reflected my moods. When I am happy they sparkle, when angry they show my anger but for those past months, they had been just hollow without emotion.

"Mum, c'mon let's go," said Jimmy.

"Nah, I'm going to do this. I need to. You go. I'll be fine."

So Jimmy left me alone in the house and I began to scrub and scrub and scrub. Washing all the germs those vile individuals left at my house. Despite feeling a bit better, having thoroughly cleaned the place, I still knew deep down in my heart that I could never ever live there again.

Paris refused to come home and had been living with her Dad. I didn't really blame her. After all, I had not been capable of looking after myself that night so how on earth could I be responsible for her wellbeing? Yes, I saved the dog but none of that seemed to matter anymore. It was not my fault yet I kept thinking that it was.

I was riddled with guilt. The amount of 'if onlys' that went through my mind on a daily basis were neverending. I contacted the housing association and they arranged for an exchange to my new home. It was only then I could finally close the chapter and begin to rebuild my life - a fresh start.

It had not only affected me but my entire family were also in pain. The boys found it hard to talk about it. They felt pretty hopeless and awkward. Paris was in pain too, and Jay was devastated because if we hadn't had the pathetic silly row, he wouldn't have gone home. A huge black cloud of despair seemed to be hanging over us all. I felt I died that horrific night and somehow now I had to overcome the hurdles. I knew it would take time and at one point even my doctor was very concerned about my welfare.

Even now, writing about this, is hard to explain exactly how I felt. There was no exact emotion, but a mixture of thousands, each appearing at different times of the day and night. When something bad happens, it is hard to see the good in the world but my children, Jay and friends were my salvation. They aided in my recovery.

I swapped the alcohol and drugs for healthy eating and joined the gymnasium. I totally lost my confidence and became anxious around groups of males. But I convinced myself that this would never happen again and slowly, little-by-little, I managed to move forward and leave the past where it belonged, in the past. I also vowed never to be that drunk and high again to cloud my judgement. Never!

Writing this has been extremely difficult for me because some anxious feelings have arisen again. I have wept so often and hopefully this is the last time I shall ever speak of this again. I want and need to rid myself of these recurring feelings because with the love from my family and friends, my life is now rebuilt. I am now proud. No longer ashamed. I have become a stronger person and learnt the hard way that life is not always fair, but we cannot let things destroy us, no matter how much we have been beaten down.

I am not particularly religious but I do believe in karma and that God moves in mysterious ways. One day, those animals will be punished for what they did, not just for revenge, but for the sake of other victims too. Nobody, be it man or woman, deserves to be raped.

After the ordeal, I received thirteen thousand five hundred pounds compensation from victim support. Clearly, they believed the truth in that case. Why didn't the jury? It sounds like a lot of money but after what I had been through, it felt like an insult. I didn't even get to spend it.

Somehow, somebody close to me stole nine thousand pounds from my bank account. You would think your money is safe in the bank, but mine wasn't. I called the police and the fraud squad were involved. Whoever did it was very conniving. They set up a PayPal account in my name, using my date of birth, my telephone number and my password, then transferred the funds to the PayPal account so it looked as though I transferred the money and it was untraceable. Only those close to me knew about the money. I don't, even to this day, know how to set up a PayPal account!

Anyway, another chapter over and now this was happening. It felt I had been violated all over again. The worse was, I knew that it was someone close to me and that hurt inside. I began mistrusting everyone, and everyone became suspects. To this day, I have no idea who it was but karma will raise its head once again. I have moved on and I am still smiling.

Chapter 29 - My babies

I grew up in the sixties and seventies. Believe me, being a child in those days was a lot different to today. I am not even talking about the technology, the mobile phones, the PlayStations and X-Boxes. I am referring to expected behaviour from us children. We were supposed to be seen and not heard.

We never dreamt of back chatting our parents without receiving a quick back hander from Dad. Even strangers used to give you a quick clip behind the ear. Dad was a good shot with the slaps and many of us used to flinch away as he struck out with the back of his hand.

We were also expected to find our own entertainment, and we did. That brings me to the subject of showing emotions. We were taught to keep everything locked up inside. To hide any doubts and fears. There wasn't any such thing as counselling and therapy. If you had a problem, you just got on with it. Usually in silence.

Although the Second World War was long finished, there was still an element of post-war Britain in the air. The Winston Churchill stiff upper lip approach, come on chaps, get on with it, no dilly dallying. We even sung a song about Hitler, which went like this.

"Hitler has only got one ball, the other is on the kitchen wall. His muvver, the dirty bugger, cut it off when he was small."

So basically, what I am trying to explain is that my generation were not taught how to express their feelings or inner emotions. Even today, I am still learning how to do that. So this chapter, I would like to say a few words about each of my six babies. Yes, I know you are all grown up now but you are always going to be Mummy's babies. So, here I go.

Damon was my first born and, being honest, he used to melt my heart. When he was about two years old he often got into mischief. But when he was told off or told "no", he would grab one of my ornaments and smash them. He was a very stubborn toddler. The little rat broke one of my favourite clowns. At a very young age, when my fence arrived to buy some stolen goods, Damon had quite clearly grasped the concept of money and tried to sell him some of his worn clothes. Needless to say the offer was declined and the disappointment on Damon's face was priceless.

So, what is he like now, Damon? He has grown into a fine young man. A very talented rapper and musician, he is followed by thousands on various social media channels. He is kind of semi-famous in the music world of today. He writes all his own material and is forever producing new songs. He lives for his music, and he loves to smoke weed, adores his dogs and is great with children. Sadly, he has none of his own but there are plenty of nieces and nephews for him to spoil.

He lives alone with his two dogs in a one bedroom flat at the heart of Kingston upon Thames. He doesn't seem to have a serious girlfriend but I know he is never short of close encounters of the women kind. A bit like his Grandad, a ladies man. He is still very stubborn but also a very loyal person - will go out of his way to help anyone in need. Aged twelve, he used to help his Grandad when he was on the dialysis machine to take out the needle and didn't bat an eyelid. There was nothing he wouldn't do for his Grandad.

He can be extremely funny but also extremely moany. He, like his Mother, has a great side but when the tables are turned, he can also be very nasty. I guess that's a trait most people have. Hell hath no fury like Damon scorned.

Sadly, Damon and I are not as close as I would like us to be. He tends to be the loner out of the six children and doesn't mix with his siblings that much. I don't think he sees much of his Dad either. I love Damon with all my heart but feel that he still resents me for not being there for him as a child. When we are together, I feel a distance between us and wish I could break down the imaginary wall he has built.

I cannot apologise for leaving him with my Dad and Maggie because I still maintain it was the right decision, but I will apologise for not being the mother that I should have been. Damon, I want you to know I am very proud of who you are and I hope that in the future we can build a closer relationship. Not just together, but with your siblings too. Mwah, Mummy loves you.

Jade was a demon of a toddler. She was a serious nightmare, super stubborn and would throw herself on the floor then proceed to head butt it. She's always been very independent and is not easily led. She made her own decisions and loves to get her own way. She is still like that today.

I remember one incident, while we were waiting for the bus when she was very small, she decided to take all her clothes off. Another time when she was older, she wanted to borrow my jeans and when I said "no", she cut off all the buttons on my leather jacket. She knew she would be in trouble but couldn't care less. That's my Jade. A very beautiful girl with amazing eyes that actually sparkle, and very content.

Nowadays, she has bloomed into a loving and devoted mother to her own five children and lives with her fiancée in Kingston upon Thames. They are due to get married this year. It may well be the wedding of the year because when Jade sets her mind to something, she usually manages to do it in style. Her entire existence is devoted to her children and puts them all first every time - going out of her way to make sure they have all the love and devotion they need.

Out of the three children I had with Gary, I suppose she is the most like his side of the family. She is a fantastic makeup artist and clever with her hands, making all the fancy dress outfits herself. So whenever her children are dressed up for school events, they usually win first prize. It's the same when she dresses up, her hair, the eye lashes and makeup are usually brilliant. I feel she could use this talent to pursue a career.

Her character is pretty loud and colourful. She loves to gossip and can chat the hind legs off a donkey. She also loves to let her hair down, party and is great fun to go out with. But I worry sometimes about her own health. She seems to have a lot of health issues for a young woman. Whenever I ask her about it, I get the standard reply, "I'm alright Mum."

She sometimes gets a bit jealous. For example, her sisters Georgie and Paris see Ricky, but she doesn't get invited to their outings. She thinks that she is being left out which is not the case. The difference is that Georgie and Paris can just pop over for a quick visit but Jade has five children to coordinate. They would never leave her out. It's just circumstances and she is very protective over Ricky because they were raised like twins. They have a close bond.

Again, there is a distance between Jade and I. I wish she would open up more to me because, despite what she thinks, I love her with all my heart and I'm very proud of her. She's a fantastic mother and probably learnt from my failings in that department. We have had plenty of fallings out over the years. Right now, I am about looking to the future and building bridges. Sometimes I see sadness in her eyes and want to protect her. So baby Jade, Mummy loves you and let us see what the future holds. I am always here for you. Out of all Gary's children, Jade has grown very fond of her Dad and I believe they have a good relationship which I am very pleased about.

Now my Rickers. As a child, he was very calm and didn't have a nasty bone in his body.

RIckkyyyyyy! Charismatic, handsome, funny. He always gets all the girls, and because of that, a lot of other men didn't like him around. He is now very settled with his partner and their two beautiful children. He has another handsome son from his first relationship and he is always with them all. He is a fantastic Dad, dotes on his children and his girlfriend. They are now his life and he provides for them all. He is generally always laughing and laid back. A bit bossy. If you cross him, he can be bitchy and very nasty with his tongue - razor sharp.

He is obsessed with fashion and actually has a page on social media where is followed by thousands to see his latest styles that he puts together. He insists that all the family wear matching outfits too. King of the styles and swagger, he is actually OCD about it and very vain. A bit too self-obsessed and will insist on twenty takes before he decides which picture to choose from.

Like all my children, he can be stubborn. Lord knows where they get that from, I say cackling with laughter. What a great cook he is too. Whenever we are invited to dine at "Chez Ricks", he always ruffles up a fantastic meal and treats you like royalty, maybe a little gift for you too. You get to eat a beautiful meal followed by a selfie with it to go on social media. Ha ha, he has a big heart.

Ricky's girlfriend is constantly reassuring me that he loves me but he is not very demonstrative and hides his feelings. But I do feel a strong bond with him. I also think that sometimes the two of them spend too much time together. Neither of them have any interests outside the family. I personally don't feel that is healthy, but hey each to their own. It seems to be working for them. Neither of them are stronger than the other. They are constantly laughing and so in love. It is a pleasure to be around them. They are very much equals in their relationship and both devils who love to party.

Ricky is a very determined young man and has the ability to achieve whatever he sets his mind to. I wish them all the best for the future. Since Dad died, Ricky assumed the male role figure of the family. All his sisters look up and respect him. He is a very strong person. He has held the family together for many years, although lately, he seems to be drifting away. I guess that happens once you have your own family to preoccupy you.

My only concern is that he and his girlfriend, party hard, maybe too hard. I don't want to sound like the pot calling the kettle black. As you know, I partied way too hard. I was fortunate enough to avoid any serious health issues, but I think Ricky needs to slow down a bit now. He is getting older and focus on his future and his beautiful family. Love you up to the moon and back, Rick!

Jimmy was estranged for many years and I finally got to meet him when he was fifteen years old. A friend of mine came and found me shopping in Kingston and said that it was time I met him. Her son was a close friend of his. They lived a few doors away from Jimmy's Nan and Grandad. So off I trotted to her house. Jade was with me and it was all very emotional. But we laughed, cried and hugged and then he became part of my life. Not only he had to deal with me being his crazy mother, he also found out he had several siblings to meet.

He is very handsome and quietly reserved. He is highly intelligent like Dad and strangely enough has a few of his traits, like pacing up and down and moaning. Once he came out of his shell, we realised that he also seems to have Dad's sense of humour and can have us in fits of the giggles.

He is now a fully qualified electrician, drives a beautiful car and still lives with his Nan and Grandad who adore him as he does them. Jimmy is very caring and worries about worrying. He loves to analyse every situation and must be

Google's best customer because he is forever researching things. He has a very inquisitive mind so we nicknamed him "Google Jimmy", which I think he prefers than "Dildo Jimmy", his previous nickname. Anyway, this young man has been through a tough journey for a young man. Yes, we have had our differences but now we seem to be on great terms and I feel close to him.

Unlike me, he cares about what people think about him. Like Ricky, he is into fashion in a big way. I secretly think he styles himself on his older brother because he admires his dress sense. But he creates his own styles too. He loves to stay fit and attends the gymnasium, has taken up jogging and cycling. That was only after a dreadful episode in his life.

At an early age, he began using drugs in a recreational manner but because he has my addictive personality, it wasn't long before the drugs controlled him. He hit rock bottom when his health took a turn for the worse - he was hospitalised. It was soul destroying to see him on self-destruct mode and fall into the abyss of the dreaded drug dealers. I despise them. But hitting rock bottom certainly gave him the kick up the arse to fight his demons. He has been clean for nine months now, and has totally turned his life around.

He likes his music and has a passion for finding the best tunes around. He seems to have a talent for this and probably would make a great Disc Jockey in his spare time. DJ Jimmy. Not that he has much free time with his fitness regime and full time work. He is now at the stage where he can be around parties and the drug scene without any desire to touch anything. It is early days and he knows it is not an easy journey, so he is taking it slowly, one day at a time. He is a very popular young man, but at the same time he likes his own space and can be a loner. He will venture out when he feels the need. He has my nasty side too but only when he is really provoked and will not tolerate bullies. It's nice to see he also has a good relationship with his Dad.

The only thing I feel saddens him is that, although he tries to establish relationships with my other children, they exclude him somewhat. They could try to include him more in their lives. What was it Dad used to instil into our brains? "Blood is thicker than water." There will always be a day when your siblings will need each other and I would rather it was now and not at my funeral.

I am so, so proud of how he managed to turn his life around. To see the difference in him is amazing. You have made me an extremely proud Mum, Jimmy boy. He hasn't got a serious girlfriend at the moment but it is great to see his confidence rebuild. The shy young fifteen year old son I met has now blossomed into a confident, very happy and funny young man.

I know Jimmy loves me. Maybe because we had to make up for so much lost time. But he accepts me for who I am and I was pretty chocked one Mother's Day when he said "I love you Mum and wouldn't change you for the world, my brilliant nutty mum." Well, I love you too Jimmy and keep up the good work. You know Mum is always here for you.

Georgie, Porgie, puddin' pie. Kissed the boys and made them cry. When the boys came out to play, Georgie Porgie ran away. Oh, if only that was the case with my Georgina. She's a live wire this one. She's on fire. The party hard, crazy girl that seems to love danger and trouble too much and worries the living daylights out of all of us. Not just me, but her siblings too. It is a worry because she has a lovely nature.

She is a stunning looking young girl who became a gymslip mother in her teenage years and was not mentally capable to take care of her daughter. History repeated itself, her Nan is raising her. Georgie lives alone in a flat in Kingston and has a crazy personality, very much larger than life. By God, she needs stabilisers to slow her down or something. She lives for the moment, is pretty useless with money, easy come easy go and her own worst enemy.

She will cause troublesome situations between people, then hide away for the rest of us to deal with. The problems, problems that she created. Although she gives out a "hard nut" persona, deep inside that is not her. It is just a false persona. Inside, she is a fragile vulnerable sixteen year old who never seems to want to grow up or face reality. She is stuck in her own little bubble and has no sense of direction or plans to move forward with her life. Because of this, I am constantly worried about what she is capable of doing next. When will she next throw herself in the path of danger?

She has been diagnosed with Borderline Personality and I am worried that she may end up losing us all. As much as we all try and help and advise her, she never ever listens! Georgie is easily influenced by people and way too trusting, naïve. I also question her sense of self-worth because she has many sexual liaisons with males and females, letting people use her and takes strangers to her home.

Outwardly, she appears a happy girl but inside I believe she is sad – promiscuous, looking for love in the wrong direction. A lost sheep. I only wish she will come to her senses and change her ways, find a career then maybe she could in the future have her daughter move in with her and become a proper mother. Georgie, please do not make the same mistakes I made.

She is forever on the internet, addicted to her phone so maybe a career in computers or even if she worked in the Vodafone shop. Just something. She is also young enough to take a course in something, train to do something with her life. Something to fill the void that obviously exists. Georgie has a great relationship with her Nan and her Dad so I am baffled at times as to why she behaves as she does.

I love my Georgie with all my heart but she puts grey hairs on my chest. She is my main worry because she will follow the crowd. She needs to be her own person. Baby girl, if you are reading this, please for your own safety try and change your ways. Mummy loves you.

Now, my baby princess, Paris. The teenage bitch from hell. Only joking, baby. The other girls were probably both the same, except I never really experienced the mood swings. Apart from a small stint with Jade, I didn't handle those very well. The blessings of living full time with a teenage daughter. Wow is that an eye opener? Teenage daughters can be such bitches, and sometimes say the nastiest most hurtful things and have no respect for their mothers. How does anyone cope? Well, sometimes, like

Elvis, I've left the building when I've had enough. It was the only way because I wanted to punch the living daylights out of her. But hey, that's my anger management and it seems to work for me.

Paris is a bit like a dumb blonde at times. That is just her age talking. Hopefully she will grow out of that. She is another one easy influenced by people and needs to express her own personality and not be a sheep. Like Jade, she is excellent with hair and makeup, very fussy with her clothes and once she has the perfect look, like Ricky, loves to take a few perfect looking selfies.

This little girl is great with kids, which is handy. When all the grandchildren visit, her nieces and nephews, she loves to cook for them. She also spends as much time as possible in her bed, a marathon sleeper if you like.

Because she is the only child that has stayed with me throughout her childhood, we have a special bond. It is not that I have a favourite, she is the baby and been with me through the good times and through the hard times. She has opened up my heart to feelings I never knew existed. She has broken my heart, worried me senseless, laughed with me, cried with me, seen me at rock bottom and helped to lift me from that dark place, twice.

At one point she hugged me and begged me to change. She supported me when there was no one else to help me and because of that probably missed out on some of her childhood. I am not particularly proud of that and feel constant guilt. It wasn't planned. It just happened.

Considering all of that, she has blossomed into a pretty normal, mood swinging, fashion conscious, phone obsessed, fun loving normal teenager - and I love her with all my heart. She is not only beautiful outside but inside too. And very loyal. If anyone crosses the loyalty line, then they are blocked, erased from her life.

She hates being indoors and loves to go out with her friends which I think is great because there are so many teenagers these days sitting at home on the internet that they develop social phobias. She can also be devious and cunning, but will go out of her way to get what she wants. Very determined, Paris will never give up - a quality that I admire about her. So my little princess Paris (that should embarrass her), Mummy loves you too.

So there you are. Six children later and many years after, I am finally trying to establish life as Mum. Having Paris with me all these years made me realise how much I missed out on all the others' lives. The feelings, the worries, the hugs, the tantrums, the kisses - all of it. But I now have to live with that.

I would like to say that I truly, with all my heart, love all my children for who they are as they are all very different people. Thankfully, they all accept me for who I am. Paris is my baby and, in time, will leave the nest so to speak, but we are enjoying life together right now.

They all have my addictive personality which is a worry of mine, but hey. I am learning. All mothers worry, it is what we do.

I feel sometimes, there is jealousy amongst some of them and between the girls. Maybe for my attention? My only wish is that we could have all the family get together, all of us. So what if there are a few arguments and squabbles amongst the children. That is a real family. Super happy families do not exist, only on the television. Let's hope I can make that happen, before my funeral!

Chapter 30 - Retirement

Having an unstable profession tended to make my home life very unstable too. I had various homes but only three ever remained in my heart because I reformed them to a high standard. My first was the three bedroomed flat I had on the Cambridge Estate with Gary, the second being the three bedroomed flat in Martin House, New Malden that I shared with Jim. The third, my pride and joy, was my three bedroomed house in Teddington. I am currently living in a lovely flat in Fulham but it's not quite up to my luxurious standards. I shall get there, little-by-little. It is very peaceful here and far away from my hometown so that people you know just don't just drop by, if you catch my drift.

You see, although I made vast amounts of money, I spent much of it - and quickly too. I seem to be not only quick in the shops, but quick in everything I do - Kim quick. I bought nice cars, furnished and renovated my home to a luxury standard, expensive holidays abroad, plastic surgery to enhance my breasts, Botox, dermal fillers, lip fillers, nail extensions, hair extensions, regular sunbeds trips and membership to the gymnasium.

My focus was purely to get money in order to lead a lavish lifestyle. Like most women, I like to pamper myself because when you look good, you feel good inside too. It boosts your happiness and self-confidence so my addiction was not only to shoplift, but also to get the 'things' I gained from doing it. These 'things' became essential to me and I could not live without them.

Reflecting back, I had way too many clothes and shoes. It was obscene and never any time to wear them because I was always shopping and my work clothes were a separate entity. My passion was to own and look after nice things. But this was also my obsession. So much so that I neglected the more important things in life, like family and relationships which, since my retirement, I am now trying to rebuild.

Since I have stopped shopping, my outlook on clothes has changed dramatically. Fashion has always been an interest of mine. These days, I haven't been very impressed with what the shops seem to offer, well not for me anyway. I guess I never really had the time to sit there and look at all the different styles because clothes were, to me, merely a commodity for my customers. I now have a desire to change my entire look and remodel myself. To dress for me and not for my shopping trips. No more work disguises. Something new and fresh. A new image which makes me excited, but I just have to be patient. I will get there.

Nowadays, I don't really have the urge to party all night but that could come with age. I think I did so much partying while younger, I no longer have the desire to do so. The drugs and alcohol that used to accompany a night out are also long behind me. My chosen drug at the moment is healthy eating and exercise. I did try going to Bingo a couple of times but gambling has never really been my thing. Besides, Bingo bored me.

I don't know what I fancy next. Maybe a night out at the opera! That would be a culture shock. I think I might even enjoy it. Who knows, maybe I shall save up for some tickets because nothing is cheap these days. Looking back at my life, I am not sure if it's a sign of the times but many years ago, people seemed genuine whereas nowadays people seem false and jealous. That is why I just keep myself to myself.

I don't miss alcohol whatsoever. In fact, I hate it. I will only have the occasional glass of red wine when out to a restaurant to accompany a nice dinner. I feel and look a helluva lot better without it and love my daily workouts I do at home. The gymnasium became too expensive and was the first thing I had to sacrifice. To be honest, it is a waste of money when you can achieve the same results from exercising at home. One thing I do know about is how to waste money.

I recently read the book The Laws of Attraction and it altered my perception on life. It was after I read it that I sat down, clearly evaluated my life and decided that I had to stop the shoplifting. Paris was also sick of the way we lived and craved for a normal lifestyle. So I took the challenge and stopped.

I have learned to manage on benefits and it is hard. But I am rising to the challenge. No more luxuries. I would love to work because I get very bored easily. With my criminal record however, it seems nobody will employ me so I find myself in a repeat of the vicious circle I experienced in my youth. There is more to me than "Kim Farry, the shoplifter", and I believe that, given the chance, I could become a great employee. I am certainly dedicated and I have staying power as my CV proves, I had one 'job' for forty six years.

I still miss Dad and wish here was here to see me making these drastic changes in my life. He would definitely be embarrassed by the media coverage. He cringed years ago when I appeared on Kilroy. I expect my siblings feel the same!

It does amuse me that, when I enter the shops, the security still proceed to follow me around. I chuckle because I know I am not about to steal anything. Idiots! I just wish Mum and Dad were here to help support me and see what I have achieved by retiring. But hey, I have my Jay.

I have always been a leader, never a sheep, and ensured that throughout my illegal career, I made sure I was not the only beneficiary from my stealing but those around me benefited too. From treating them to lavish restaurants to throwing boat and house parties. Whenever I held a bash, I always footed the bill for everyone. Nobody had to sum with funds because it was my treat. I loved to spoil people and why not? Life is short, enjoy it while you can.

I have six children and I love each and everyone of them. We have our fallings out, but that is just being part of any family. I could have chosen to raise them all but then, when I was imprisoned, they would have been farmed out to family members or - worse still - sucked into the foster system. I knew I was living an unstable lifestyle so chose to ensure they remained with family members that could provide them with the stability I couldn't.

Fuck, it wasn't easy to walk away from them but it was the right decision to make. I never ever stopped loving them nor thinking about them. They have all done me proud and turned out pretty well. An added bonus is they have provided me with some beautiful grandchildren. So, I am now a Nanny and making up for lost time by spoiling them.

I chose to keep Paris and guess have tried my hardest with her. She is now eighteen and still living with me. It really was because of her I decided to finally stop shoplifting. She is evolving into a beautiful young woman who, don't get me wrong, like all teenagers, she has her moments too. It is strange for me to experience the emotional teenager because I never had that with the other children. Seeing her upset makes me upset. I am finally experiencing what it is like to be an active Mum and actually find myself enjoying it. I do regret missing out on the other children's lives. You cannot turn the clocks back, no matter how much you want to.

All my children know I would kill for any one of them. We are making up for lost time and they know who I truly am. I can be funny, crazy, cranky, angry, happy and sad. Just like any other human being. Although, my crankiness is probably a bit crankier than others. I am not made of stone. I have emotions like anyone else. I feel hurt and pain, yet I am very good at hiding it behind a huge smile - those childhood acting classes.

Since giving up shoplifting - or should I say, hanging up my shopping bags - I feel as though part of me has died. That is the only way I can describe it. Shopping ruled my life and gave me the feeling of security, power, happiness and love. I felt invincible and in control of all the shops, hundreds of them. I was my own boss. The Boss. I wish I could think of a legal way to run a legitimate company because I know inside me, I have the skills to do so. I just need to come up with an idea.

I will not lie, I miss the shop lifting terribly. The clothes, the buzz, and the luxuries. Getting what I wanted, when I wanted it. I also miss that I can no longer spoil others when they are down on their luck. No more Kimmy to the rescue like I used to be. I would quickly run to the shops and return with goodies to brighten people's day. People that were struggling with poverty, I loved to make them happy and that is the buzz I miss the most. The buzz of going to work and meeting up with my clients. I miss that immensely like you wouldn't believe. It pulls at me far stronger than when I gave up nicotine. I am constantly fighting the urge to shop everyday. My brain was constantly ticking away with new ideas to scam the shops and still does it today. But I have to try and switch it off by distracting myself.

How I miss the money and the routine of shopping. Being the boss of my own business, feeling important, having a vast list of clients relying on me. Now, sometimes, I have barely any food in my cupboards and unsure if I have enough gas and electricity to last the week. I also walk everywhere because I cannot afford public transport. I am now doing daily home workouts and OCD cleaning my flat.

I still manage to see the funny side of life and joke about where I now am. The real plus side is that I am spending far more time with my children and they all agree that I have become a much better person, having given up the shoplifting. That counteracts all the shopping bags in the world. I am so lucky that they accept me and love me for who I am, and not who I was.

By writing this book, I am trying to show people that it is never too late to turn your life around. Whether you are suffering from an addiction, in an abusive relationship or just in a shitty job where no one appreciates you, you can turn your life around and make that change. If I did it, anyone can. It has been two years since I last stole anything and the journey has been tough to say the least. Leaving aside the mental cravings, I had to learn to live on the poverty line.

No more extravagant Christmases, it is more like Tiny Tim's Christmas. Yet, I have learned from this experience that 'the things' are just that – things - and they don't really matter. What is important is good health, family, friends and feeling happy.

None of us know where we will be in the future, or what the future holds. But I am not a quitter and currently fighting this addiction daily. One day at a time, and it is early days, I have to keep going and stay strong. What I have experienced in my lifetime, it is no wonder I am made of iron. Please believe me when I say I feel stronger than ever. My mind feels clear so I shall crack on.

Since I chose to go public in the media, I have seen many people judge me. The main thing is that people believe because I chose to shoplift, therefore, I am a bad person which I assure you is not the case. Some of the comments made have been hurtful, but I am pretty thick skinned so I tend to forget about them quickly. I chose to go public because I wanted to better myself and thought, by getting my face everywhere, I would be shamed into staying straight. I am very proud of who I am today. I know that I am limited edition. There is no one else quite like me, be that good or bad.

I did used to have some funny times during my shopping and admit I was pretty greedy. My saying used to be, "Somebody stop me!" - followed by my cackle of laughter. I had to have things done my way and confess to being a complete control freak.

I am far happier right now than I have ever been, despite the financial hardship. I love my daily workouts, cleaning my home and preparing fresh healthy meals on a budget. My values in life are no longer topsy-turvy. I can see clearly now the clouds of shopping have been removed. Having my family makes me the richest lady in the world; things that money cannot buy are what is important. Time and happiness.

I feel like I have already been to hell and back but right now I am in a very happy place. A good place. I am finally able to laugh again. Laughter has an incredible power to cure most things. My infectious cackle has returned and that is a good sign because for a while it disappeared. But now, it is back! My life has been a long and rocky road but I wouldn't change a thing. Everything I've experienced has made me the person I am today. Right now, I am quite happy with "me". My only regret is that I was not a better mother to my children.

I hope this book has given you an insight into who I am and not just "The Shameless

Shoplifter" which the media branded me. The media (I now know) put words into my mouth that I'd never say, and print lies, so now is my chance to set the record straight. I admit to being a thief and there are far more thieves out there with far less morals than I had. I never harmed any other human being, just dented a hole in the shops' profits. I am also willing to help anyone who has an addiction because my struggle was hard. Being a kleptomaniac is not easy, but I shall overcome this.

Throughout my life as a serial shoplifter, I have always maintained that by stealing from shops, I was not harming anyone. Yet since I have stopped, I now know different. My addiction to shopping caused me to hurt many people, those that loved me, even myself. For that, I am truly sorry. Committing crime means doing time, not just in prison but also mentally. I was torturing myself, doing time inside my head. No amount of money can change that. Only I can. Was it all worth it, NO!

I think I could be a bit like Marmite. You either love me or hate me. The thing is, I am who I am and finally enjoying my life with my banging boobs and daily workouts. One thing is for sure - you can never keep me down for long. I always see the funny side of life. Sink or swim, and I am definitely a strong swimmer. As Dory sings, "Just keep swimming…"

Now you all know the truth, I am off to cook a banging dinner. So, live life to the full and make sure you fill it with a lot of laughter. "Byeeee…" (cackle).

"The last chapter of your life has not been written yet. You hold the pen. Write the story you want to read in the end."

26162054R00163

Printed in Great Britain
by Amazon